Cover Design by Danielle Lampman

Unless otherwise noted, all scripture quotations from the *Holy Bible*, King James Version, public domain in USA.

Scripture passages marked RSV have been taken from the Revised Standard Version of the Bible, copyright © 1946, 1952, and 1971 the Division of Christian Education of the National Council of the Churches of Christ in the United States of America. Used by permission. All rights reserved.

Scripture quotations marked (AMP) are taken from the Amplified Bible, Copyright © 2015 by The Lockman Foundation. Used by permission.

To order bulk copies of this book, please contact the publishers, Derek & Sonia McLeod via email at derekandsonia@gmail.com
Visit the website www.mynehemiahwall.com

ISBN *(Print)*: 979-8-9903766-0-1
ISBN *(E-Book)*: 979-8-9903766-1-8

First Printing, 2024.
Printed in the United States of America.

TEACH ME TO WAR

What Others Are Saying

"*Teach Me To War* has opened up a topic that is shameful for a lot of people to admit. This is not shared often in churches; it's a subject not spoken of. This book is going to bring deliverance to people and encouragement, hope, and peace to those in torment and condemnation." ~ C. Mooswa

"This book was such an encouragement and it will steal every heart that reads it and bring them to the source! It will restore and heal the broken. It was by far the most anointed, and amazing book I have ever read." ~ B. Ince

"*Teach Me To War* should be on the desk of every biblical, marriage and family counsellor. This book will shake, break, convict, and most importantly give you hope. It teaches you how to stand in adversity and go to war for your loved ones. Sonia is a mighty warrior, her husband was right in saying "You are an intercessor, a repairer of the breach." All glory to the Lord. This is His masterpiece." ~ D. Lampman

"I wasn't able to put this book down. With raw honesty this couple allowed the reader to visualize and walk this journey with them. This book is a must read for any married couple. It is a testament to what God can do in a marriage and the faithfulness of a praying wife. Whatever path you may be on, this book will be a blessing and a healing help to you." - *D. Doucette*

"*Teach Me To War* is a powerful and deeply inspiring book. Through vulnerable storytelling and raw honesty, Sonia navigates us through the complexities of betrayal, forgiveness, and ultimately, redemption, showcasing the transformative power of faith and prayer in overcoming seemingly insurmountable obstacles. This book serves as a beacon of hope for couples facing similar challenges, offering a compelling narrative of God's amazing grace and the restoration power of love in the midst of brokenness." - *N. Guidos*

TEACH ME TO WAR

SONIA GWEN MCLEOD
DEREK MCLEOD

Derek & Sonia McLeod

And that he died for all, that they which live should not henceforth live unto themselves, but unto him which died for them, and rose again.
2 Corinthians 5:15

Dedication

I dedicate this to the wife who wants to give up because she has been hurt and wounded by her husband's wandering eyes. There is hope for you and for your marriage.

This is for the husband who desires freedom. This is for the man who self-loathes and sees no way out. Although it may seem impossible there is freedom for you. This is for those who are trying to live a godly life but find themselves enslaved in sin.

This is for those who are backslidden and feel like it is too late for them. It is not too late! You can return to the Lord. He loves you and is waiting for you. Return to Him with all your heart.

Acknowledgment

I want to acknowledge my husband and best friend, Derek. I love you with all my heart. I greatly respect all you do for us and our family and I admire your strength. Thank you for your transparency and opening your heart to help others in their battles. I understand why the enemy has tried so hard to destroy you time and time again.

Thank you to all our children for inspiring me to keep going. Our children, Hassan(Phoebe), Hasslina, David and Joshua, Kari(Sylvain), Karyl(Roland), and Kirsten.

To my mother, Joy. Derek and I are so very grateful for your steadfast faith, your love, and your encouragement. You have always held firm in your belief that the Lord was at work in our lives and had a great calling on us. Thank you for *always* being there for us. And, of course, my baby sisters: Kendra, Shaneequa, and Sky.

To the families of *Times Square Church – Summit Campus, Summit International School of Ministry*, Pastor Carter Conlon, Pastors Pavel and Hailey Maftey, Pastor Josiah DeRoos, and all the TSC leaders. We could not have made it without you and the gracious hospitality you all gave.

I must also include Becky from Canada, and Bruce and Amy from Mechanicsburg, PA, who also stepped in to help us. We can't thank you enough for taking the time out of your day to come, serve, and feed us. Your love and encouragement brought hope to our hearts.

Pastor Larry Keegstra, we witnessed firsthand your faithfulness and service for the Lord and it has been a great encouragement to our own ministry. Thank you.

Thank you also to Matthew & Sibi Washington; Torrey & Gloria Antone; Cindy & Gustavo Guzman; Andrew & Danielle Lampman; Norma Guidos; and Doreen Doucette.

And finally, thank you to all of our friends, co-workers, and the many guests of Bethesda Mission.

Contents

Introduction

Our prayer and hope is that this book, *Teach Me To War*, will inspire and encourage you to keep praying for your families and marriages. Our story is one of triumph and victory, but it could have been much different. We are in a spiritual war and if we are ignorant and unaware of our position in Christ, we stand to lose what the Lord has given us. We have an enemy who wants to destroy our families, our homes, and our marriages. But through Christ we are more than conquerors. The Lord will move in ways we may not understand but He is always in our midst.

When I met Derek, I met my best friend. I was networking for my book, *Rise Up My Beloved*, when I received an email from him. I posted my book release on a Christian site and he saw it and felt compelled to respond to me. He thought it was cool and exciting to see a First Nations author. He said it was my smile and my glowing face that drew him. He wanted to have what he saw in me. What he saw was the joy and love that I had for my Savior Jesus Christ.

I remember the email and the first time I saw his picture, my thought was that he looked dark and had a lot going on inside of him. Nonetheless, I replied to him. After exchanging a few emails, we chatted on the phone. I called him and from our first conversation, it felt like we had been friends our whole life. There was a connection between us that we both immediately felt. We had both come from failed marriages and we each had a desire to marry again.

On May 15, 2010, I married my best friend. We are now going on 14 years and we know that the Lord has directed us to share our story with you. Glean what you can from our story and leave behind what you want. Our story is about pain and triumph. We have cried together and have been pressed on all sides. Our hope is to be an encouragement to others who are struggling and suffering in silence.

Be encouraged in your battle right now because He knows what you are enduring and He is working it all out for your good. The Lord wants every part of our heart surrendered, every stone turned, and every crevice cleaned out. Let nothing hinder what He desires to do in your life.

Prologue

"I can't do this anymore! I don't want to be married to him anymore Lord!! I was angry and humiliated. I felt justified in my anger.

My heart was wounded. As the hot tears ran down my cheeks, I ran to the Lord to take refuge in Him. It was at that moment that He spoke these words to me: *"My people do this to me everyday, they run to other places and they break my heart."* I had never seen how we so easily forget about Him and run to other places and things for comfort. I was guilty of running to other places other than to Him. My heart was pierced. I had hurt the Lord with my own selfishness. It was in this time that the Lord showed me the story of Hosea and his harlot wife, Gomer.

When I first heard the story of Hosea I wondered about it because I didn't quite understand it. What was the message we needed to hear from it? What was the Lord speaking? Now here I was and the revelation of Hosea was being opened to my eyes.

If you're unfamiliar with the story, it goes like this: God told Hosea to marry a harlot and to have children with her. '"Go, take to yourself a wife of whoredom and have children of whoredom, for the land commits great whoredom by forsaking the Lord.'" (Hosea 1:2).

Israel had broken their covenant with God. And so, to speak to the nation of Israel, He used the marriage of the prophet Hosea and his harlot wife, Gomer. Like her, Israel had played the harlot with God.

When Hosea married Gomer, it would have been shocking to those who knew him. He was a well-respected man of God. She was a prostitute and, according to the law, she was unclean. Undoubtedly, others around him frowned upon his choice to marry a woman like Gomer. But why would God tell him to marry a harlot? That did not make sense to do that. Certainly, there must have been someone better than her to marry. But their love story is a powerful illustration of the Lord's incredible divine love toward us.

Through this the Lord demonstrates how we play the harlot. He wanted to reveal His judgment and mercy through the prophet's life and marriage. Hosea's life was on full display to send Israel a message. The nation of Israel had broken their covenant with the Lord God Jehovah. Hosea is instructed to name his children that would speak of God's coming judgments. When Gomer returns to her worldly lovers, God tells Hosea to go after her. In His love for her, the Lord intervenes time after time to stop her from going to them. This is a story that symbolizes our relationship with God.

We are like Gomer and her whorish ways. We are the ones that play the harlot. That may seem harsh, but it is the truth. Our love for the Lord has waned, and we have pursued other ways. We have found other pleasures and we have grieved Him.

His blessings are in front of us and we're surrounded by His goodness. He does this so we would run back to Him. How many times have you heard His Word or had someone speak life to you in a moment you needed it? Look around you and you will see His blessings.

My husband and I have put everything down, our reputations and our lives. Our lives are not our own, but they belong to Him. And the life that we now live is for Him who died for us and rose again. (2 Corinthians 5:15)

If we want deliverance in our lives, we need to bring to light what is hidden in darkness.

We hope you will find encouragement and strength in knowing that you are not alone in your struggle and that the Lord moves in hard places. He has brought us through and has shown Himself strong on our behalf. As you read our story, our prayer is that your heart falls passionately in love with Jesus.

PART ONE

Go And Marry a Harlot

The beginning of the word of the Lord by Hosea.
And the Lord said to Hosea, Go, take unto thee a wife of whoredoms and
children of whoredoms: for the land hath committed great whoredom,
departing from the Lord.
Hosea 1:2

One

The Day He Left

November 2017

I don't remember how the argument started, but it was the day everything changed.

It was a regular day at home. The boys may have been playing in the backyard, or running around inside the house. They were five and six years old, just eleven months apart, and full of energy. They loved playing with toys, building blocks, and their pets. We had a German Shepherd dog named Nikki and a cat named Chewie. We had a busy household. Derek may have been watching TV, and I was probably tackling the housework. But it didn't take much for us to get into a full-scale fight anymore. I knew something drastic needed to happen in our marriage before it changed for the better. We always ended up back in the same arguments about his wandering eyes and how much it wounded my heart. There was too much hurt over the years. I had been praying for deliverance from the spirit of lust for my husband for years, and nothing was changing. The hard part was knowing that I was aware about his struggle before we got married. Yet, his honesty and transparency had me believing that the situation couldn't be that bad. We had the Lord on our side! And He was bigger and stronger than any enemy that stood in front of us. But the answer to deliverance from lust never came. And the pain that came with it was more than I could have imagined. I didn't know on that day that the catalyst for that change would take place. I found myself saying the words I swore I'd never say again to my husband. I yelled at him, "Get out!"

The hurt, anger and bitterness had shut my eyes to the love and promises of God for my marriage. I saw no future with this man who thought only of himself. I had become cynical and was tired of what, to me, seemed to be his lies.

I knew the cycle, I would confront him about looking at another woman, he would get angry, deny it and become defensive. The argument would start but it was pointless because he wasn't hearing me. I began to resent him because we didn't do much anymore together. Forget about going shopping with him! We didn't take the chance of going anywhere too busy because we knew someone would catch his eye, and I would feel the hurt all over again. I had this one haunting memory that broke me every time it came to my mind. It would also be the same time the Lord would speak to my heart about His own wounded heart and how He understood my pain. I was not alone in my betrayal.

My husband and I were on the road to a two-day conference hosted by Pure Life Ministries. It was for men who wanted freedom over lust and who had been bound to pornography. Derek wanted to go to it because he wanted freedom. It seemed promising, and it looked like the answer we had been waiting for so we were hopeful and excited. We hit the road and we were eager for this road trip.

I remember my husband wearing a white dress shirt that day, making him stand out. The white color of his shirt brought out his dark eyes, which I loved. I had a handsome husband. He made me feel like a schoolgirl again. Deliverance was going to finally come!

We had to stop at a Walmart to grab a few things for the road and for our stay at the motel. I needed toiletries and snacks for that evening. At the store checkout, we saw an attractive blonde packing her groceries over in the next aisle. It didn't take long before my husband noticed her, and she noticed him. They stared at each other as if they were the only ones in the room. I could feel the hurt rising inside of me. I looked at my husband to turn to acknowledge me, but he didn't. He completely forgot about me. I looked at her, and then she looked at me and I could see that she realized he was with someone. That was the painful part when you watch your husband flirt in front of you with no regard for you or your marriage. We paid and bagged our snacks, and as we headed towards the door, I yelled at him, "Go on and go home with her!" I told him he was free to go. And as far as I was concerned, he could stay with her. I wanted nothing to do with him. I told him the next time he saw someone he liked, I could help get the woman's number for him.

I hated him at that moment and I didn't want to be around him. When we got to the vehicle, I sat in the back seat. I didn't want to be anywhere near him. I could feel the hot tears running down my cheeks. How could he say he loved me? There was no honor or respect for me. He had no regard for me as his wife. His arrogance and lust for other women cut me to the core. Couldn't he see the woman of God that stood beside him? "I can't do this anymore! I don't want to be married to him anymore, Lord!!" I screamed inside. "This hurts too much. He has no honor for me and I don't deserve this. I'm done. He can be alone and go back to being a womanizer!" I was angry and humiliated. I felt justified in my anger and didn't want to be married anymore. My heart was broken and wounded.

I ran to the Lord to take refuge in Him. It was at that moment He spoke these words to me: *"My people do this to me everyday, they run to other places and they break my heart."* His words shook and sobered me to the core. I had never seen how we so easily forget about Him and run to other places and things for comfort. My heart was pierced. I had hurt the Lord with my own selfishness. He laid His life down for us on the cross when He didn't have to so that we could live. He paid a price we could not pay. We all had played the harlot. I was guilty of running to other places other than to Him at times. I felt pierced in my own heart of how I had hurt the Lord in my own selfishness. *Forgive me Lord, and help me to forgive my husband.* He poured out grace and I felt love and compassion for him. I had to push on in my marriage. I wasn't alone in my heartbreak, and the Lord was acquainted with me in all my suffering. He knew what I was feeling. My husband wouldn't go outside of our marriage, I was sure of that, but there was a reason why the Lord said that if you look upon another with lust, you have committed adultery. No one wanted their husband looking at another with lust in his eyes for her.

King Solomon had 700 wives and 300 concubines, and that's baffling to fathom, but it's easy for men to have that many, and more, in their imaginations. I knew what was happening through the lens of my husband's eyes and the images that would follow. This battle with lust was ongoing, and the enemy never seemed far in his ways to lure and seduce. He waited outside the door. We didn't do much as a family anymore and I felt like I was becoming a prisoner. It was safer to stay at home than to be assaulted each time with a new face and a new incident with another woman. I knew attractive women were everywhere, and I couldn't compete with those I saw. I wanted to be the only woman that got my husband's attention. There were two things that we did as a family; go for supper and go for an afternoon drive. Whenever we got to a restaurant, I focused on the boys, the menu and ordering food. But I could sense when the spirit of lust was trying to grab my husband's attention. If any women were sitting nearby, my husband would definitely notice. I could feel my-self literally shake inside at those moments. I was noticing however that he was getting better at keeping his eyes on me and showing me honor as his wife.

It's been years of struggling with lust in our marriage. How much longer, Lord? Our biggest problem was him taking responsibility for it and praying about it. When I brought it up, he would get angry and defensive. He didn't think I knew his eyes were taking in more than they should. I knew he had a hard time praying. Whenever we prayed together, I could feel something wasn't right. I didn't under-stand what was going on and I had no clue. I knew he wanted to follow the Lord and wanted freedom. But by this time, I knew the pattern. He would be okay for a day or two in his pursuit of follow-ing the Lord, and then he would fall into bondage to the sin of lust. He wasn't watching porn anymore, at least not to my knowledge. It was a result of the pornography that he had habitually watched for many years before. Through pornography, the spirit of lust had built a stronghold. As a consequence, the women he saw would arouse and entice him with sexual imaginations and imagery.

Studies have shown that watching porn releases a chemical in the brain called dopamine. It also causes the brain to remember these vivid memories to relive that stimulation. It makes a person feel good and it becomes like a drug to them. It is much like being addicted to heroin.

A big part of my frustration was that he couldn't pray. He could pray for our food, and in church, but there was no shutting in with the Lord. I knew freedom was on the other side of prayer if he would only pray. Did he really want freedom? Why couldn't he obey? Did he want to get close to the Lord? It made me angry that he could have me as his wife, to serve him food, take care of our home, and do all that I did for him, while he continued on in his sin. It just did not seem fair.

Derek struggled with depression and suicidal thoughts. At times it would overwhelm him. I remember one night when I didn't know what to do, I just spoke the Word over him. I recalled all the memory verses that I had memorized and spoke them over him. It helped him and lifted him up. But he would fall into this same place over and over again.

I would watch my husband go in and out of depression. He often stayed there for several days, and it was hard to watch him endure that. I knew he was being kicked around and lied to by the enemy. He saw himself as worthless and said it would be better for everyone if he weren't around. I loved my husband despite his weaknesses. We all have weaknesses and fall short of the glory of God. On the flip side, behind this battle with lust, was a humorous, caring, compassionate man, a good provider, and I felt protected and secure with him. It hurt inside and angered me that he couldn't believe the word for himself. He was a wonderful man and he was my best friend. I could talk to him about everything and anything. He's the guy that opens my car door and still brings me flowers. When I wake up, he brings me a cup of coffee with toast. My happiness has been his pursuit, but he was bound to something stronger than he was, and we needed help. I couldn't endure the hurt anymore.

After I kicked him out and he left the house that day, I figured that as he had done before, he would be back home in a couple of hours. But this time, there was no sign of him, not even a text or call from him. When I tried to call his phone, there was no answer. I didn't know that he had boarded a bus and had left the city. He had no intention of coming back. I checked our bank account, and nothing could tell me where he could be. We didn't have much money in the bank to begin with. I had a sick feeling in my stomach that he left us for good or that he would try to hurt himself.

I thought of places that he could go to, and I thought of my stepdaughter in Ottawa. He had a daughter living there who was attending college. I messaged her, and she confirmed to me he was there. He had gone completely across the province! A couple of days later, he finally called me. But he wouldn't give me an address because he knew I would have packed up the boys and drove to see him. His response to me was cold. I tried to talk to him, but what he said next sent shivers down my spine. He told me he was looking for a new place and a new job. He stated that he was planning to start his life over again. I couldn't believe what he was saying to me. This wasn't the same Derek that I knew. This wasn't the same man that I married. He spoke so coldly to me. 'You can't be serious?!' I thought, but I knew he was. I had already experienced the pain of abandonment in my first marriage, and I couldn't believe I was facing this again. My heart sank, and my body shook. I had seen him turn his back on other people when they got him upset. It was my turn, and I was going to feel the pain from the rejection that stemmed from a deep wound that he was carrying. There was no way that I was going to reach what was deep down inside his heart.

Derek

Since birth, I've been different. I was born in a helicopter, miles away from any city or town. My godparents were the attending nurse and the helicopter pilot. My first childhood memory is like a faded black-and-white film. I am sitting on a bed, and loud noises awaken me. Suddenly, two people come crashing through the door fighting. I faintly recall my baby sister lying on the bed beside me. I may have been around two or three years old at the time. At that young age, my home was filled with alcohol and violence. But soon, my mom and dad made Jesus Christ their Lord and Savior. And it forever changed our home, our lives, and our community.

At a young age, I loved Jesus. I invited my cousins to church. I took pictures with my index finger held up to indicate that there was only one way — Jesus! In fact, at a very tender age, I led my grand-uncle (probably in his mid-60s) to the Lord. I loved Jesus!

But as I grew older, I became the target of many bullies, including adults who held positions of authority. They hated the gospel. And to them, I was the child of the local preacher, so I was an easy target. It didn't help that I was intelligent and a bright student who liked talking. I was a nerd and it made me a bigger target. Before long, I began to resent constantly being bullied and started fighting back. I hated being different. I was different because I was a preacher's son. I was different because I wasn't Indian enough for some and too Indian for others. I entered my pre-teens and adolescence with a wounded heart. I only wanted to be left alone and to blend in. But I did not realize that this mark of being 'different' had been put on my life by God, who had plans for my life that I knew nothing about.

On August 4, 1990, at approximately 11:00 p.m., I called on Jesus to save me. And He did. From head to toe, I experienced His cleansing power over my life. I was gloriously saved. And I loved the Lord with all my heart, but the wounds and the hurts from my youth were still present. I immaturely married at a young age and to an unbeliever. I struggled for many years to follow the Lord. I fell over and over again. And then, during the March Break weekend of 2007, I was broken and in deep dark despair. I knew I had nowhere else to go, except to the Lord. He called me back, and I made my decision to follow Him. Despite my deep desire for the Lord, I still carried many wounds and immense hurt. I was in a very dark place. But the Lord had plans for me.

One year later, in the late summer of 2008, I was in an online Christian forum and saw this Native author promoting her book, *Rise Up My Beloved*. She was beautiful and radiant! It was her smile that first captured and captivated me. That smile was an incredible ray of light into the dark dungeon of my heart. There was life in her. She exuded a joy that I longed for in my depressing existence. I had always wanted to write a book. And to see that she had authored a book as a First Nation woman – a Christian First Nation woman – made me want to reach out to her. But all the years of hurt, pain, and wounds kept me from reaching out. Voices rose in my head, "She will never respond to you! Who are you? You're nothing and no one! Why even bother saying anything? You're out of her league, and she will never look your way!" I felt so little and worthless. But the thought rose up in me that even if she never responded to me, I had to tell her how cool it was that she had written a book! And so, I wrote a few short sentences to let her know what I thought of her amazing achievement.

And I never got a response – until about a month and a half

later. I was absolutely shocked, yet elated and ecstatic that she had responded! I don't recall many details of the emails we exchanged over the next few days or weeks, but soon enough, we transitioned to using MSN Messenger (remember those days?) to communicate. Eventually, we took the bold step of speaking on the phone. As cheesy as it sounds, the moment we first spoke on the phone, it was as if we had known each other our whole lives! And yet, in our case, it was absolutely true. And the rest, as they say, is history. And we've been making history and memories ever since.

Two

A New Start

London, Ontario - 2008

I was back in London, Ontario and it never felt so good. The plan was to come back for a visit to bring my two children for visitation with their other parents. But once I got back into the province, I knew that this was where I wanted to be. I moved into a three-story walk-up apartment and it was in an area of London that I knew and was happy to live in. I got a job at Value Village. I worked production in the back of the store and enjoyed working there. It was a job and I had employee discounts for clothing that helped me out. I was a single mother of two again. I wanted to go back to school for social work. The *House of Rahab* was still a vision that I was pursuing; a Christian-based drug rehabilitation center that would house and help women bound to drugs and alcohol. I carried a burden for those who were struggling and hurting. I knew all about the struggle of addictions having been there myself. The memory of the rundown crack houses and being on the streets are still a vivid reminder of hopelessness. I never could have imagined that my life was going to turn around to give the Lord glory. I never imagined that I would write a book.

I was in total despair before Jesus came into my life. There was hope in Jesus Christ. I had known "Christians" before and had no desire to become one of them. I didn't feel good enough to become one. But now that I had personally experienced the mercy, grace, power and love of God, there was no going back to who, or what, I once was before Christ. If I knew one thing, it's not the *"do's and don'ts"* that keep a person on the straight and narrow, but it's love and intimacy with Him that does. I was running after my Lord and Savior, Jesus Christ, with all that I had. I couldn't make it in the coming days if I didn't stay close to him.

My primary focus was promoting my book, *Rise Up My Beloved.* I was networking for my book on different Christian forums. I had finally finished the book that the Lord had placed on my heart to write before previously leaving Ontario to head to Saskatchewan. I had no idea my writing was going to be in "real time" to record the things I would go through in the months that followed.

I remember when I lived in Eckville, Alberta in 2007. My whole world had just fallen apart. My mother was with me and was home for the week. She worked at one of the oil rigs as a Cook. One evening as she sat across from me, I sat there crying uncontrollably and she asked me what was wrong. I couldn't give her an answer. I was grieving two major losses in my life. My marriage was done and I had just lost my grandmother. My own family rejected me. How was I supposed to go on living? A lie began to penetrate my mind that since I had dedicated my life to the Lord, things had only worsened. It wanted me to question what good had come from serving Him.

I had left Ontario to look after my grandmother in Saskatchewan who passed away August 10, 2005. Her name was Gwen Crane. She was beautiful and a woman of great strength. I once told her that I was there to help her because there "is only one Gwen Crane." She replied back to me, "No, there are two." And she was right, I was named after her. I see the significance behind that name now because she was a voice and an advocate. She was a strong voice and she stood to bring change for Indigenous peoples. She was the first native female chief in Canada. In a similar way, I am following after her footsteps by being a voice for the Lord and pushing through despite the obstacles. The Lord brought me through a dark time in my life. I knew He would one day use the pain and things I endured to help and encourage others. David the psalmist wrote these words that resonate deep in my heart:

> If I ascend up into heaven, thou art there: if I make my bed in hell, behold, thou art there. (Psalm 139:8).

No matter how far we have gone, or how badly we think we may have messed up, the Lord is there for us.

Maybe you are in the same position. You know that the Lord has called you to stand for truth. He has called you to stand for injustice. I think of Queen Esther, she risked her life by approaching the king without being summoned because there was a plan to destroy the Jewish people. She risked her own life to save others. Her uncle urged her to tell the king and reminded her that she was here for such a time as this. In our present time, evil is trying to silence God's truth. Now is our time to stand for truth. Everything you have gone through has been for a purpose and for a much greater plan. There are evil plans in motion right now, and yet, the gospel has to be told. Will you take a stand like Esther? There are people in your family and your community who are watching your life right now. Your stand for the gospel will compel others to follow. The places He takes us are not easy, but He equips us for every season.

For a brief period, before coming back to London, Ontario, I lived in my dad's community of Cowessess, a small First Nation reservation in Saskatchewan. I didn't want to go out there because I wasn't close to my dad or that side of the family. I wanted to get out of Saskatchewan as quickly as possible because of everything that had taken place (*which I detail in my book Rise Up My Beloved*), but I didn't have the finances to do that. The community was building new houses and, on my dad's advice, I submitted an application for one. I was living in a one-bedroom apartment with my mom and my children at this time. Because I was basically homeless, I was approved for one of the new houses. I was excited and scared. The thought of being on a reserve where I didn't know anyone wasn't appealing to me. My home reserve was Key First Nation and I had only recently transferred my membership over to Cowessess First Nation. My hope was to eventually move back to Ontario. But I went because the Lord had made it clear to me that I was to go.

My daughter had the cutest little cat. I don't remember his name, but he was adorable. He was all white and had quickly become my daughter's closest friend. She did everything with this cat. Her cat loved to have baths and I've not known another cat like hers since. Whenever Hasslina had a bath, her cat would jump right into the bathtub with her. My daughter was in kindergarten and she was having a rough start of her school year and settling in. Her cat was her comfort and he adored her too.

Some time later, I was invited to my paternal brother's wedding in Saskatoon. That was a couple hours of driving and it meant that I would be home very late. When we arrived back it was about 4:00 a.m. I was exhausted and the kids were asleep when we arrived home. As we came through the front door, Hasslina's cat darted outside. I was too tired to go outside and look for the cat. That was a mistake.

It was around 6:00 a.m. and, in my sleepy state, I vaguely recalled hearing dogs barking outside. This was weird because I didn't have neighbors with dogs. Most dogs just roamed around the reservation.

I fell back asleep and was abruptly awoken by my daughter who was standing there crying. She told me her cat was dead and it was in the front yard. My heart fell and I jumped out of bed and ran to the front window and there it was laying in the yard. I now understood why the dogs were barking earlier that morning. I was half asleep and didn't know what was happening. I went and grabbed my girl and we cried together. I felt her shaking as she sobbed in my arms. I yelled for my son to get outside and to pick up her cat. I told him to throw it in a garbage bag until I could figure out what to do. I was upset and angry. I went to my bedroom, fell on my bed and began to cry out to the Lord, "Why Lord? Why did you let this happen? Why? This cat was my daughter's only friend." She was traumatized by what had happened. I had not wanted to go to that community. I found myself wondering why I was there in the first place.

When I left the house later that evening, I saw his tiny little paw prints on the front door. He must have taken refuge under the deck but the dogs drove him out. And when he made it to the door, he was mauled. My heart hurt seeing that and I was upset with myself that I had dismissed the barking.

As I cried out to the Lord in my bedroom, the Lord spoke this verse to my heart that His people are counted as sheep for the slaughter.

As it is written, For thy sake we are killed all the day long; we are accounted as sheep for the slaughter.(Romans 8:36).

The Lord showed me an image of His people coming to the house of God in search of hope and healing, but they could not find any. Instead they were turned away. Many left the Lord's house feeling lost and rejected. They were treated as castaways. As they came to the doors of the church, they did not find the truth. The shepherds who once had a zeal for the Lord had turned from the truth. And many today have become like Eli and his sons. His sons would entice and seduce the women who came to the temple. When his sons took the best of the meat offerings that were brought to the temple, Eli would enjoy the prepared meat with his sons. They had no love or concern for the people. Today, many are lost because there are no more shepherds in the house weeping over their sins. I stopped crying because this hit me to the core. I was crying for one cat that cut me to the heart, but His heart is wounded for all those who come to His church and never receive life or healing. He grieves for those who have been destroyed and for those who cannot find comfort and love from those who should have shown them the most love.

The Lord gave me a dream that spoke to me about the coldness of people's hearts.

In the dream, I was walking up and down the aisles of a library. I had this intense overwhelming feeling in my heart that the Lord was revealing to me how His Word was no longer changing hearts and convicting people. When I came down the last aisle I saw a table. At the table sat a preacher that I knew was loved by many people. When I got to him I began to tell him the burden upon my heart. I told him how I felt the Lord was grieved that the Word of God was no longer changing people. And this preacher who others referred to as "The Walking Bible" began to quote scriptures. I didn't have the chance to say much more to him before he would interrupt and begin talking again. He knew the Word of God, but had stopped listening to it. The preacher in my dream, "The Walking Bible", died tragically. He died while driving impaired. Recently, another well-known preacher, who was also highly esteemed, passed away. After his death things began to surface that he had been doing in secret. He had been heavily engrossed in pornography and had committed adultery with many women. Many were shocked and left reeling from the news.

There is a lot that happens in the church that no one wants to talk about, but our time is almost up. We will answer for how we lived and how we represented Him on the earth. We are living in the last days. We have been given a short time to turn and yield to His word and to examine our hearts. We are to walk as He walked and to love as He loves.

If it wasn't for the warning and dreams I had before leaving Ontario, maybe I would have succumbed to the lie that my life was over.

I had three dreams before leaving for Saskatchewan. In the first dream, I was looking out my townhouse bedroom window. In the near distance, I could see dark, billowing clouds coming toward me. I wasn't afraid in my dream, but I knew there was a storm coming. I went to my pastor at that time and he told me that the dream was meant for me and that I needed to pray.

In the second dream, I was in a large stadium. I was standing on a platform as I was getting ready to share God's Word. As I began to speak, I could hear chairs moving and people began leaving the stadium.

I was in a school auditorium in the third dream. Once again as I got up to speak, people began leaving the gym. I asked a family member who was also the pastor of the church I attended for the interpretation. He told me that when the Lord began to use me, I would lose family and friends. Ironically, he would be the first to walk away from me.

One Sunday morning while he was ministering a sermon, he spoke over my life that the Lord would give me hinds' feet to put me in places that I never thought I would go. He was right. It wasn't a physical place that he was referring to, but a spiritual place. The Lord would raise me up above the storm that was to come. I would have opposition, but the Lord would keep me as a testimony.

Now here I was back in Ontario, and by the Lord's mercies, I had not been consumed. I was not destroyed. I was bruised, but I was healing. It was a new season. I had completed my book and I was seeing the beauty rising from the ashes. Testimony after testimony came from those who read my book and said that they couldn't put it down. The Lord was faithful and I could clearly see the hand of God upon my life.

Genesis 50:20 But as for you, ye thought evil against me; but God meant it unto good, to bring to pass, as it is this day, to save much people alive.

Joseph spoke these words to his brothers. The same ones who had sold him into slavery and had hoped to be rid of him forever. Joseph was greatly hated by his siblings. They couldn't stand him because he was favored and was the most loved by their father. Yet, he had forgiven them and he saw how God had worked through it all. There were times I could see my life in the story of Joseph in how he overcame incredible odds to bring hope. There is a purpose and plan in all that we go through. We have two options in times of adversity, we can hand it over to the Lord for Him to use for His glory, or we can become bitter and give up.

Just like you and I, Joseph dealt with everyday feelings and emotions. We can be sure that he probably often wondered why his life had not gone how he had hoped. The plans we have for our lives may seem derailed but if we persevere the Lord has a bigger plan for our lives. The enemy had tried to kill and destroy Joseph, but the Lord took the evil that was used against him and turned it for good. He had endured the suffering which turned out to be preparation for what God put in his hand. He became second in command over all of Egypt and saved many people when famine hit the land, including the siblings who tried to kill him. He was saved to save many people! What may look like death to you is only the beginning of what the Lord wants to do through you. And it is never for your sake only, but it is almost always for the sake of saving many others.

You may be hated and your circumstances may be out of control. They may not make any sense right now but He is in the midst and is doing something. Like Joseph, it's learning to trust Him despite what is happening. You were wonderfully formed in your mother's womb and preserved for an incredible purpose. He is the redeemer and restorer of all things. He makes all things new. If you are in the same place of being misunderstood and rejected by those you love, take comfort in knowing that you are in good company. I felt hated by a few of my siblings and I was not received by family members, but the Heavenly Father loved me. Like Joseph, the Lord has His hand on me. It is for a divine purpose as well. Regardless of who you have been rejected by, just know that the Lord has not forsaken you. He has incredible plans for your life.

The Word was written for our admonition and for our instruction (1 Corinthians 10:13). We see the characteristics of the men and women that the Lord used mightily like Esther, Nehemiah, and Gideon to name a few. These names will be mentioned a little later on. We will see their weaknesses and learn from their experiences. They endured pain and had wounds in their hearts like we do and in their darkest times they continued looking to God. We must do the same.

I was picking up a few things for supper at the grocery store one afternoon and I could feel the hair on my head flopping around. I had it up in a messy bun with no care in the world at that moment. I stopped caring about what I looked like and I knew I couldn't do that anymore. I needed to take care of myself. I wanted to get married again and the thought occurred to me that I could potentially bump into him in one of the grocery aisles for all I knew. I had seen enough chick flicks back in the day and read enough true love magazines to know that meeting a guy could happen anywhere. I had to be ready at all times. What my guy was going to look like didn't concern me as much as it did what he was on the inside. I wanted my husband to know the word of God like I knew how to stock my food pantry. He had to know His Word. If I was going to feed him good stir fry, I wanted him to feed me a good word from God's truth.

I focused on my job at Value Village and my children. My oldest, Hassan, was in grade eight and my youngest daughter Hasslina was in grade three. They were growing up fast and I knew that serving the Lord was the best thing I could give to them. My children were my reasons to persevere and the Lord was using them to keep me on the narrow road. I wasn't going to follow the crowds, or do what other people were doing, and I didn't want my children to do that either. At the end of the day, I understood what mattered most: the choices I made for my children. Although I was a single parent, I decided, that "as for me and my house, we will serve the Lord" (Joshua 24:15).I understood that the broad way was the way to destruction and there were many people going that way. I was done with the drinking and the way I used to live. I knew the path to Jesus Christ was a narrow road and only a few found it.

I had a friend who called one day because she had found out that I was a Christian now. It's funny how quickly news spreads. I told her the rumor was right. I was serving the Lord now and I was no longer going to the clubs. She told me, "You're not missing anything. Everyone is swapping partners." That's the only thing I remember from the whole conversation.

The kids' school was within walking distance, which made things easy. Hassan had his first paper route job. That was good, it gave us something to do. Once a week we piled up the newspapers on our cart and we delivered newspapers down the street. We stayed busy and I prayed with the kids in the evenings. I was comforted that Jesus was in our home. We came through a rough season and were looking forward to a new one.

One afternoon I headed over to the plaza to do some shopping. I remember the Lord speaking to my heart on the way there about guarding my testimony. I knew the enemy wasn't going to leave me alone; he was after my faith to destroy it. I had just finished writing a book and if he could ruin that testimony there would be none. I was back in a familiar place, my old stomping grounds. As I walked into the grocery store a lady walked right in front of me, literally cutting me off! She almost hit me and she didn't apologize, but kept on walking like nothing happened. Well, that wasn't nice! I said something to her and she said something back. I was mad and before I had time to even think about it, I said to her, "Come again?!" Then I remembered His words! And I felt convicted. What if the woman came back? I blew it and my testimony could have been marred. I was thankful to the Lord that nothing happened more than it did. I heard a saying before and it stuck with me. A teacher who has been working hard with his students all year is rewarded when they do well on his exam. It shows if his students have been listening in class. I knew He was going to test me with His Word and with the instruction that He gave me. I knew what to do, but would I do it?

Watch and pray, that ye enter not into temptation: the spirit indeed is willing, but the flesh is weak. (Matthew 26:4)

The carnal nature which ruled my life before Jesus Christ would try to poke its head out again. No, I couldn't do anything in my own strength and I was no match for the enemy.

The carnal spirit lives by the lust of the flesh, lust of the eyes, and the pride of life (1John 2:16). It seeks to do its own thing and goes against the Spirit of God. It is in rebellion to the Holy Spirit. And the only way we overcome this carnal nature is by reading His Word to renew the mind and by yielding to the Holy Spirit. We must obey His Word so that our faith can abound and grow. My children watched everything I do and I had to lead by example.

I went into the secondhand store to pick up material for my

curtains. After leaving the checkout, I stopped outside the doors to look at my receipt. There was an error in what I had paid. The amount I paid was less than what I should have paid. I saw that the cashier had only charged me for one drape instead of two. I went back into the store and told the cashier the mistake she made and I paid the difference. She thanked me for being honest. I had to be honest in the small things. I knew the Lord was with me everywhere I went. The kids were with me and I knew they were watching.

On another trip to the plaza, my kids and I went running to the dollar store because it was almost closing time. The kids managed to get in but before I could go in one of the store's employees held out her arm to stop me from going inside. I glared at her and said, "Don't put your hands on me!" Right then, I saw my daughter at the checkout. She had been watching the exchange between myself and the employee. My response towards the employee made my little girl react the same way I did. She turned to the employee and started making mad faces at her. And it was in that moment that the Lord showed me that I had to lead by example because my daughter would follow my lead. I didn't want my daughter to learn to fight conflicts with aggression. I did that my whole life, and I knew that fighting wasn't the answer.

Our battle is not with flesh and blood but with principalities and powers in high places (Ephesians 6:12). There is a spiritual war being waged against us. In those moments, the enemy wanted me to fight with my words so that he could beat me with them later. My other choice was to walk in love and do the right thing because the Lord wanted me to do what He would do. I was going to wear humility. I was not going back to being that hard cold person I was before.

That day, I walked over to the young girl and I apologized to her. Immediately, I noticed she dropped her guard and became respectful and warm. I know she was just doing her job. That small act of kindness ended that hostility and my daughter saw the exchange.

Her face wasn't distorted and angry now but was happier. I could see it on her and she was smiling again. On our way home, I told her that I had been wrong and that I had to say sorry to the girl who was working there. She was only doing her job and I had to do mine.

There is joy in the heart when we do what's pleasing in His sight. When we fall into sin, it feels horrible. 'Change my heart Lord and don't leave me the same' has been my life's prayer. And He has answered it time and time again for me.

Sanctification of our lives through God's Word takes time. It has to prune our hearts. I have found the Holy Spirit to be tender as He breaks down the hard places of our hearts. I had finished my book, *Rise Up My Beloved*, and I would be tested on the Word of God that was given to me. Through the life of the prophet Jeremiah, the Lord would show me the process He would use to mold and make me.

We read in Jeremiah 18 that the Word of the Lord came to Jeremiah and told him to go down to the potter's house and there the Lord would give him a message. When he got there he saw that the potter held a piece of clay in his hand. He placed that clay on the potter's wheel. Jeremiah watched as the potter began to form it into another piece. And he continued doing this until he was pleased with his work. The Lord told Jeremiah that this is what He desired from him and the nation of Israel. The Lord wanted to do His work in their hearts so that he could make them pleasing in His sight.

He still desires to do this in the hearts of His people today.

There was a fire in my bones to share God's Word and declare what He had done for me. If I had any doubts before that the calling of God was on my life, I no longer had any doubts. I had written about my deliverance from out of the miry pit, from the hold of alcohol and drugs, and from all kinds of other filth. I knew the Lord was with me, and He was not finished with me yet. He has always had a purpose and a plan for my life. Ever since I was 16, my mother told me that there was a calling upon my life. As a young mother, only 15 years of age, she remembers holding me as a baby. Looking down on me, the Lord spoke to her heart that He was going to use my life to minister to many lives. As a rebellious teenager, I had a hard time believing my mother's words. My dad was 17 at that time and he had gone on to Bible College. My mom had no desire to be a preacher's wife. But when I met my Lord and Savior I knew what my mother had said was true; I was going to tell the whole world about Him and what He did for me in my life. My eyes were on a harvest of souls. His love will cause you to do things you never imagined yourself doing.

* * *

Fall 2008

One day, I received an email from a guy named Derek. He had seen my book release online and thought it was cool to see a Christian native author. He knew he had to send me a message to at least say 'hello.' After a few emails, he said he knew my dad, Melvin Stevenson. Derek told me that he heard him preach in his community before. He even told me that we were cousins. I called my mom feeling disappointed, and asked her if she knew if I had any relatives in Moose Factory. But she responded 'No, we have no relatives over there.' This guy Derek sure had a sense of humor. He had me laughing.

We started talking on messenger, way before Facebook came along. I remember changing my settings to play a song by *The Kry*, "*I'll Find You There*", every time he came online. And without fail, every time I heard that song play, my heart would race and I would come running to the computer. This guy had something different about him. I felt like I was 16 years old again.

This was the beginning of getting to know one another. We stayed up some nights talking on the phone until the sun came up, talking about our lives and what we both wanted to do with it. We were like a couple of school kids again. One thing was clear: our love for the Lord. We talked about the Lord all the time. It meant so much to me having someone who knew the Word of God like he did. He was polite and caring. He was considerate and respectful.

One day, as we were talking on messenger, I told him that I would send him a video. I wanted to send him a video of myself saying 'Hi!' with a little wave. That was it. A little while later he sent back a five-minute video of himself that left me in tears crying from laughing. He pretended to be a host on a radio station taking questions on air about the book, *Rise Up My Beloved* by author Sonia Crane. He legitimately played the part of a real online radio host. At one point, he pretended to take a call from an older man, who said "If I was any younger, I would be chasing her down. I'm 70. She's a – what do you young people say? – she's a hottie!" He then closed his video by saying to his audience, "Remember, wherever you are, that's where you'll be!" He had me hooked. I couldn't wait to meet him, but it would have to be in God's timing. He lived on an island and he would need to take a helicopter, train, and vehicle to come see me.

A short while later, I needed to run some errands. As I stepped out of the apartment building and came to the parking lot, my car was gone. My car had been stolen! I went back inside my apartment and called the police. I was told by neighbors that we had drug addicts in our building and the assumption was that they took my vehicle. When I called the police back they informed me that my car had been found and it had now been impounded. I didn't have the money to get it out of the impound yard because it was $50 for each day that it was there. It wasn't worth paying the fees to get it out. The front end had a hole in the floor and since the repairs would cost a lot more than the fees they wanted, I left the car there. We needed another car and we had to trust the Lord to get us another one. The kids and I started using the city transportation and it proved to be a challenge. I was going to miss my vehicle, that was for sure. The Lord poured out His grace because I needed it to handle what had happened and to endure going without a vehicle. Although it was a major inconvenience, I told the kids we were not going to complain. We had much to be thankful for. In the midst of it all, He gave me strength and contentment to go without a vehicle. I told the kids that we were going to experience what many other people had to go through. We were going to walk, and take the bus, like others had to do.

You might be going through a difficult time, and everything may be feeling hopeless, but He will carry you through the season. Trust Him in this season, and you will reap the reward for your obedience and faithfulness. There may be losses but the Lord knows how to provide and restore!

I knew I had an enemy who wanted nothing more than for me to quit and relinquish what the Lord had done for me. I had to keep pushing through.

Winter moved in over the next several weeks, and it got cold. It became rough when the kids and I had to run for buses, or when the buses were behind schedule. Weeks went by and then one day, I got an unexpected phone call. It was from a couple in the Lord who had read my book. They were friendly, warm and excited to meet me. I agreed to meet with them. It was encouraging to know that my book was bringing forth fruit and that it was a blessing to those who read it. We met at a local coffee shop which was just around the corner from where I lived. They were a wonderful older couple and we had a good time in fellowship.

A few weeks later they called again and said they were coming to see me and they had something for me. A time to meet was arranged and I wondered what they had for me. I was standing at the entrance to my apartment building waiting for them to arrive. This time when they came, they traveled in two vehicles. One vehicle I knew was theirs, but the second vehicle was a Nissan Sentra. I could not believe it because I immediately knew they were bringing it to me. What was most incredible of it all was that it was the same make and model as the one my grandmother had. It was the one I would drive when I would take her to her appointments. Even the interior was the same as her car! I knew that only the Lord could have done this. It wasn't until a couple of days later, as I was out driving it around, that I was struck and overwhelmed by it all. I started crying when I realized what the Lord had done for me. I knew He had given this car to me because of my obedience to Him.

It all meant so much more when I thought back to my time in Saskatchewan. Although it may have been done unintentionally, I was deeply hurt by my family at my grandmother's funeral.

I was not included in any part of the funeral ceremony. I knew my grandmother would have wanted me to have a part. I gave up everything in Ontario to go down and care for her when she needed help. After everything that had been done by my family, would I yield and forgive when I was hurt and angry? Yes, I could and I did. But it was something that I could not have done in my own strength. I wanted to get angry and lash back. But I was without excuse. I had a relationship with Jesus Christ. I could be in the presence of God! And like a child that runs to their father, I ran to Him in tears and released the hurt. In return, He gave me grace and love for them. All the anger and pain was washed away. I didn't feel it anymore, it was gone. It was only the Lord who held me during that time. And the blessing had come because I surrendered everything over to Him. My family didn't know Jesus Christ and they were not saved. I was the one born again and redeemed.

It is because what Jesus did for me on the cross of Calvary that my sins are forgiven. He died for me and took away all the judgments that were against me. Those that had hurt me didn't know Him nor His love. I knew the truth and I had to walk in it. When I accepted Jesus Christ in my life, He changed me. I had the Spirit of the Living

God dwelling inside of me. I now had a new life in Christ. The old was passed away and all things had now become new (2 Corinthians 5:17). He translated me out of darkness and into light (1 Peter 2:9). His Word says that we are seated with Him in heavenly places (Ephesians 2:6). He carries us above the storms. We are going to go through trials, but He said be of good cheer because He overcame all things(John 16:33). I couldn't harden my heart against them.

This was the second vehicle the Lord had blessed me with. Both times I told no one that I needed a vehicle. The Lord's provision was evident. I never had a car payment as a single parent. The next time we spoke, I told Derek what happened and he was surprised. I told him, "I must be going somewhere." And I did.

Three

Heading North

Spring 2009

I made an appointment at the local college in London to inquire about taking Social Work. The school counselor said they had no open spots for the Social Work program that I wanted in London until the following year. That was too long to wait and I needed to look elsewhere. I was told that there were available spots in Northern Ontario. I would have to do an exam as a mature student since I didn't have a grade twelve diploma, or a GED. This was going to be a move by faith because I didn't know anyone in Northern Ontario. But if the Lord wanted me there, He would make a way for us to move there. I knew that staying at my current position at Value Village was not an option.

The day came when I had to take the exam to enter the Social Work program as a mature student. It was going to have to be the Lord to help me pass this exam. I got stuck on a comprehension question. I remember looking out the window, tapping my fingers on the desk, saying to the Lord, 'this has to be all you. I can't do this exam alone.' I completed the exam and left feeling very nervous about getting a passing grade. Once again, the Lord made a way. I was overjoyed when I learned that I had passed the entry exam! I was very surprised, to say the least.

I registered online at Northern College in Timmins, Ontario. I didn't know anyone in that city. But one Christian couple that I had sent my book to a few weeks before, lived in a small town called Cochrane which was about 45 minutes from Timmins. I had never met them but I decided to tell them that I was heading north to Timmins. They offered me to stay at their place while my children and I looked for a place to live. Things were falling into place.

When we got to Timmins, I went to check in at the college office for my upcoming classes. My heart sank when I was informed that I wasn't registered to that campus, but to Contact North. Confused, I asked the receptionist, "What is Contact North?" She told me that they were online classes for those who lived in the surrounding area which also happened to include Cochrane, the town I was staying in for the weekend. I still had the option to attend classes on campus but I had to check to see if there was room in each of the classes I was registered in. Now I was unsure what to do. I drove to a plaza near the campus and checked the community board for apartments to rent. I found none. The plaza was busy, so I asked a couple of people in passing if they knew of any apartments for rent. They knew of none. Timmins had a zero-vacancy rate they added. I drove up and down several more streets and quickly got discouraged. I decided to head back to Cochrane before it got dark. Northern Ontario is dense with forest and wild animals, so it could be hazardous.

When I got back to Cochrane, I explained what happened to Agnes, the lady that I was staying with. She seemed happy about it and suggested that I find a place there in Cochrane. She and her husband pastored a church and I know she was hoping that I would move closer to help them in some capacity at their church. I decided

I would look at Cochrane since I was registered to Contact North. The couple that I was staying with seemed like the nicest people. My kids weren't entirely happy about moving to a smaller town but at this point, we needed a place. The next day I got up and scouted up and down the streets. I couldn't find anything. Lord, I thought you wanted me here? I was beginning to doubt the entire move and wondered if I had done the right thing. Maybe the Lord didn't want me here.

I went back to her house and told her I didn't find anything. We had lunch, coffee and fellowshipped some more before she suggested I go out and look again. I had to keep looking. I believed that this was where the Lord wanted me to be. I didn't want to panic. It had taken me eight hours to drive here and everything else had seemed to fall into place. As I came up a street, I saw an Indigenous woman outside an apartment. I pulled over and called out to her and she came over. I asked her if she knew of any available apartments in the area and she told me yes, her son was moving from the upper apartment to the first floor and that the upstairs apartment would be available. Finally, some good news. She went inside and came back with a contact number for me. I went back to Agnes' house feeling encouraged and called the number. They weren't scheduled to show the apartment until the following week, but I told the lady who answered that I needed to see it by 11:00 a.m. the next morning. I had to head back to London.

Shortly before I was planning to leave, the landlord called and agreed to meet me at the apartment! I headed over and I immediately fell in love with the place. It had hardwood floors with French doors. It was super cute and I loved it. I told him that I was a student and that I only had a couple hundred dollars for a deposit. To my surprise, he said 'Ok.' And just like that the apartment was mine. We were moving to Cochrane!

The guy that I had been talking to on the phone for the past several months was going to be really close by. I knew Derek was relocating and getting ready to move to Cochrane too. We had stopped talking for several weeks now because we were having some minor disagreements. He knew that I was moving to Timmins for school. He had no idea I was moving to Cochrane. The idea of meeting him and being nearer to him made me nervous. From the first conversation we had we knew there was something definitely there between us. We were like teenagers and talked all hours of the night.

I love the story of how I met my husband and how he tells it. His face always lights up when he talks about it. He was drawn to me because of the joy on my face. He saw life in me and he wanted that for himself. He said that there was no feeling of lust for me because what he saw in me went deeper than that. This is why he needed to message me. It was the fragrance of Jesus Christ in my life that compelled him to me. And it would be the same fragrance that attracted my husband now.

There were a few things on my "list" that I asked him about in the beginning that were important to me. The first one was to find out if he mixed in any native ceremonial with the Christian faith.

I did not mix my faith and firmly believe that when we receive Jesus Christ as our personal savior, all things become new. And our identity is found in Jesus Christ. My life was hidden in Jesus Christ and the life that I live now was not mine, but my faith was in the Son of God, who gave His life for me and rose again. He does not share His glory.

Derek did not mix the two either. It was also important to me that my husband-to-be knew the Word of God and could feed me spiritually. After going through a divorce and becoming an outcast from my own family's church, I had to find a heart that loved Jesus Christ with all their heart. I desired someone who was completely given over to Him. It would be even better if he knew of Times Square Church in New York City and knew of David Wilkerson.

Finding a man who served the Lord with all their heart was attractive. A man who searched the scriptures and lived by them was one to be found! Pursuing someone for their looks, or what they drove, or what they did for a living seemed superficial to me. I wanted someone who would be there for the long haul and who I could build my life with.

I decided I was going to ask Derek about a specific Bible verse that I didn't understand and see if he could explain it to me. I didn't have long to wait since we talked everyday. The following day, I asked him and he said he was up at 5:00 a.m. that morning and God was showing him what that exact word meant. I thought he was just trying to make a good impression on me. But the zeal and passion I heard in his voice convinced me that he was telling the truth. It was surreal how things were happening between us. And the last thing I wanted to know was if he knew of Times Square Church. His response was shocking and exciting. He not only knew of Times Square Church, and the late David Wilkerson, but he personally had met the TSC's Senior Pastor, Carter Conlon, many years before when he ministered in one of the Cree communities of James Bay. It would also be a time when one of the local leaders rebuked Carter Conlon. After that service, Derek went over to go sit and talk with Carter Conlon to encourage him. He said he felt bad for what had taken place and was embarrassed about what happened. I was surprised and happy that we seemed to be in agreement on many things.

Derek's honesty and heart is what spoke to mine. He put some things on the table that he struggled with but only one, I wondered about. He said he struggled with lust. I remember thinking that this wasn't going to be easy but because of his honesty, I knew in Christ we could overcome this together. But I had no idea of the intense pain and trauma that would come later down the road.

Four

We Finally Meet

Fall 2009

Derek called me one day and asked if I was moving to Cochrane. He and his mother had bumped into Agnes when they travelled south from his community to do some shopping. Agnes had told him the news that I was moving there and that I would be joining them in their fellowship. I explained to Derek that I didn't arrange this move intentionally. It was completely by accident. It was crazy how things were turning out. We were both moving to the same town and would be serving in the same fellowship. It was at this point we started talking again.

I had started my classes with Contact North and was settling into my little apartment. It would be only a couple of weeks later that Derek would make his move to Cochrane. We would end up meeting for the first time at Agnes' home. The day for Derek's arrival was here. I was nervous about meeting him. What if I didn't like him? What if there wasn't an attraction? He had my heart already. I spent the evening with Agnes and knew that Derek would be coming in on the train that evening. His train didn't come in until around 9:00 p.m. so I had the evening to wait. We talked before he left Moose Factory for the train and he told me that when he saw me, he was going to give me a big hug.

Well, the time finally arrived. I was soon to meet the guy I had been talking to on the phone all this time. Agnes sent me to her room to try on some clothes she had. From the back bedroom I heard them coming in. It was Agnes' husband Jim, Derek, and his daughter. He had a daughter the same age as mine and I knew she was coming too. I tried to stall as long as I could. I could hear Agnes greeting them at the door. And then I heard his voice. That voice that I loved to hear. The one I waited on each day to hear was here in the flesh! I freaked out.

There was no room for me to run anywhere. It was time to meet Mr. McLeod face-to-face. I exited the bedroom and headed down the hall. There he was, watching me as I came into the kitchen. He was wearing a striped grey and black shirt and, just as he promised, he came over and gave me a big hug. This was the moment we both had been waiting for. It would always be memorable for us both. When he gave me my hug, a heavy dose of body odor came with it. He almost knocked me over! It was evidence that told me he was sweating bullets on the train and that he hadn't put on any deodorant. We still laugh at that moment. It was funny back then, and it's still funny now. He still kicks himself because he forgot to wear deodorant for a five-hour train ride to meet a woman he was nervous to meet. We sat down at the kitchen table to talk and I could tell he was more nervous than I was. His daughter looked like her daddy and she had a warm bubbly personality that was easy to fall in love with. I couldn't wait for our daughters to meet. This was the beginning of our relationship.

He stayed at a bed and breakfast with his daughter for a few weeks until he was able to find a place in town. We attended the same church. He sang and did worship music. That's what I loved the most about him. He had a passion to sing for the Lord. I loved that he could play the guitar. And I loved his voice.

After a few weeks, he finally got an apartment in town. I was plugging away at my first year of social work in my online classes. I was enjoying them and it wasn't as difficult as I thought it would be to learn online. In the evenings Derek and I would go for a walk or out for a drive. We knew it was probably not a good idea to be alone, but we both ignored it thinking that because we were both adults we would be fine. But it wouldn't be long before we gave in to sexual temptation.

One evening, Derek and I went for a drive as we would normally do. As we sat parked in a small park just on the outskirts of town, we saw a police cruiser pull in. The police officer came over to my window. I put my window down and he asked if we were ok. I told him that everything was ok but my voice came out sounding shaky. I felt like he could detect my lewd thoughts and what our intentions were. It definitely felt like they knew that being alone together wasn't a good thing. It was as if the Lord was sending His "spiritual officers" to remind us that sin was lurking at the door. But our lust overcame us and it wasn't long before we fell into sin. Since we both served in leadership roles, we knew we needed to be accountable for our actions. We both stepped down from our roles in the church.

Brothers and sisters, please keep yourselves pure until your wedding night. We have always regretted what we did and we know it robbed us of the joy it could have brought into the marriage had we waited and walked in obedience to the Lord. I wonder now how much more the Lord would have blessed our marriage if we had stayed obedient and waited.

The problem in the beginning of our relationship should have made me run from him, but I cared for him. I loved how he loved the Lord. We could talk for hours and it was like I had known him my whole life. I understand that some might say it sounds corny, but it's the truth. I knew he struggled with some deep issues. I noticed that when we had a disagreement he would shut me out. He would stop talking to me and avoid me. He would pull the blinds on his window and lay in bed for a couple of days. When he didn't answer my calls or texts, I would head over to his place. What is going on? And why is he doing this? I became relentless in getting him out of that dark room. I would knock on his window and door, wondering 'What is wrong with this guy?' I didn't understand. He was a Christian, but I wasn't seeing any fruit. I just knew however, that I couldn't leave him like that.

There were moments where a dark presence would blanket his room and our conversations. Then he would confess that he had fallen back into pornography. I would get angry but I knew it had to be a decision for him to seek the Lord about. It hurt but that was between him and the Lord. Did I think that this would not be an issue after we got married? I pushed the thought out of my mind and didn't think about it. I knew that there would be problems but I also knew what the Lord had done for me and in my heart. We had the Lord and because of that, I believed and trusted that we would be ok.

Spring 2010

Things moved along between Derek and I. Our relationship got closer and closer. Derek was struggling financially because the contract he had been working on was completed and he needed to find work. We knew that we wanted to get married, but he had no money for an engagement ring. He was praying that the Lord would make a way for him to buy it. Derek once worked for an Indigenous employment agency that had an office in Cochrane. One day, he received an email asking if he would consider facilitating a resume course. They needed to spend the rest of the money for the year-end and he was asked to put a resume workshop together. He put it together and submitted his proposal with his asking price. And they gave it to him! I didn't know at the time but it was just enough for the engagement ring that he had his eyes on for me. Of course, I had no idea about any of this until after our engagement.

Derek told me that his sister asked him to do a favor and to pick up a bike for her son in town. He wanted me to go with him. When we got to the mall, he headed toward the Zellers. I went to the bathroom and back out to the vehicle to wait for him. As I was waiting, my door swung open and Derek was standing there. He took my hand to help me get out of the vehicle. When I got out, Derek got down on one knee in a small puddle of rain. He was holding a solitaire diamond ring in his hand. "Sonia, will you marry me?" he asked. And without any hesitation, I said "Yes! I will marry you." I knew I was marrying my best friend. My ring was beautiful! And the whole bike story was made up so he could surprise me with my engagement ring.

We were now engaged and I knew that all of our lives were going to change. One afternoon, as I walked around the lake in Cochrane, I stopped on the bridge to look over the water. I remember feeling a sadness come over my heart knowing that my intimacy with the Lord was going to be different. I knew that I would no longer be alone with Him like I had before. I would serve my husband and my house. We would walk as one and the Lord would become the main cord in our threefold cord.

We had both been married before and adultery was the reason for divorce in both of our situations. We knew that we wouldn't be received in some Christian circles because of what they believed. Some believed that we wouldn't make heaven our home because we were remarried and that hell would be our eternal destination. I would have to question their faith in Christ, because if one is walking in Him, they would know that He is full of mercy. Although the Lord has no desire to see marriages broken, He allowed grounds for divorce when a spouse committed adultery. And we had peace in our hearts about getting married. We were going to honor the Lord in it and keep Him in the forefront of our marriage. We have seen how marriages today are being destroyed and they are not taken seriously anymore. Sadly, most marriages now only last a few years.

We don't condone getting a divorce and we strongly believe in fighting for your marriage. If you're married, and your spouse has committed adultery, you have grounds for divorce. But it is not encouraged, and our hope is that your marriage would be restored and reconciled, because the Lord is able to heal and restore that marriage. God still hates divorce. In both our situations, they did not want reconciliation.

When we had our problems in the beginning of our relationship, the Lord spoke to my heart to stop speaking to other people about Derek and vice versa. When we did this it gave the other person the wrong impression of our spouse. They would form their own opinions and this wasn't fair to him, or to me. We both stopped turning to other people and turned to one another. Love covers a multitude of sins.

Derek may have seemed like a hard guy on the outside, but he had a tenderness and gentleness about him. I remember asking him if he was romantic. Who doesn't like romance? I may have read too many of those true love story magazines that my mother used to read growing up. I wanted an occasional candle-lit dinner, a man who opened my doors, a guy who brought me flowers from time to time and said sweet things to me. I wanted an old-fashioned kinda guy. But he answered me by saying that the most romantic thing he would do was to sit and watch a movie with me. 'What!? Are you serious!?' He said he was set in his ways.

It didn't matter what he told me about his life, my feelings for him only deepened. He listened to my heart and always had a word that encouraged me. I was drawn to him because of how he endured and pressed onward in his faith. He held onto the Lord when his youngest brother's body was ravaged and taken by cancer. Or when he faced deep battles with depression and suicide, he would hold on and trust in the Lord. The bouts of depression that would come were not easy. He told me that he could see a picture of a noose and the thoughts of killing himself came on very strong. Derek endured a lot and he was still here pressing onward. Yet, with everything he revealed to me, as bad as they all were, I grew more and more in love with him.

One evening, he invited me out for dinner. This dinner date was one for the books (no pun intended). It would rank as one of my most embarrassing moments I ever had. We went to a steakhouse restaurant and after we finished our main course, dessert came out. I could not pass up the chocolate cake on the menu. I was enjoying my piece of cake and after several bites, Derek asked me, "Do you always eat like that?" I said, "What do you mean? " He said, "Every time you take a bite from your cake you close your eyes," and he began to imitate what I would do. I could feel my face get hot and I wanted to sink through the floor! 'What? No way!! He has to be kidding me.' I went in to eat another piece of cake and I could feel my eyes close the moment the chocolate hit my mouth. Why did that happen to me? I was not aware of that at all. How long had I been doing that before? Days, months, years?? Oh my goodness. To this day, this still happens.

I've been an animal lover for as long as I can remember, and I've always been surrounded by animals. When I was a little girl, I lived with my grandmother and we had a dog named Zar. He stayed in a crib in the basement at the foot of the stairs. And whenever I would come in through the back door, he would be jumping up and down to come and see me. He was like a toddler and my playmate until one day he was out on the road traveling with my grandmother. They got stuck in a severe storm and when she opened the door, he ran out onto the road and was killed by a transport truck. That was my first heartbreak over an animal.

We always had a pet and at the time of meeting Derek, we had a cat named Dorothy. But because of his oldest daughter who had allergies and how he felt about them being in the house, I decided to re-home her. I got her fixed and, fortunately, we found her a good home.

I had talked with other Christian guys before I started talking to Derek and had no problem ending the relationship before it got started. Then there was his name and middle name. He thought I was a prophet because I guessed his middle name. But even more bizarre was his name. I told him that there was something about "his name." And I sensed something profound and strong about it. I told him several times, "There's something different about your name." I know now it was because I was the "one" who would carry his name. But we would both learn of a deeper reason behind his name years later and it stunned us both.

There is a small tourist stop outside of Cochrane that Derek and I would often go and sit. The first time we stopped there we got out to walk. It was here that Derek told me that when he saw me walking ahead of him, he felt a strong desire just to hold my hand. There wasn't anything sexual behind it, but he just had that urge just to hold my hand and walk with me. This was a huge moment for Derek. He was not a guy for holding hands with anyone before because he thought it was corny. It was then he realized just how deep his feelings were for me. He knew that this was different than anything else he had ever known.

May 15, 2010

We got married in Cochrane in northern Ontario. A beautiful small lake laid in the middle of town. It had a beautiful bandstand

and a pathway that circled the park. It was one of the main attractions of the town. Nearby was a small restaurant that we would often go to that served the best poutine and fries. The people were warm and friendly. We couldn't have asked for a more perfect place. It was the town where we met and where we served in the same church. Cochrane was where everyone coming out of northern Ontario by rail would disembark and head out to points south and elsewhere. It was where Derek and I first met and where we would now become one. The Lord had brought us here and He was now launching us into a new chapter of our lives together.

The day before our wedding the weather called for a storm. It was supposed to rain but the day turned out perfect. My wedding dress was perfect and it had a long train like how I always wanted to have. Our daughters were our flower girls. We chose black and red for our wedding colors. My bridesmaid was my friend Cheryl, and Derek's best man was his friend, Mike. We had our hall beautifully decorated for dinner. There were a few mishaps that I wish I could do over, like dying my hair a few days before my wedding rather than the night before. I had black dye on my hand at the altar that my husband asked me about later. My flower girls didn't have the rose petals we had bought for the day. We completely forgot about them but I never noticed until much later. I'm not sure if anyone noticed but if they did no one said anything.

I was hoping my dad would surprise me and show up at my wedding. I had called and asked him to do what fathers usually do, but I didn't hear from him. So, I turned to the ones who rightfully held that role: my mother and my oldest son. Hassan walked me halfway to the altar and my mom walked me the rest of the way. The ceremony was very special. My husband looked exceptionally handsome in his dress suit. As our Pastor performed the wedding ceremony, we could sense the spirit of God and even the Pastor began to get emotional as we proclaimed our vows to one another.

When the time came to give each other our rings we knew the Lord was present with us. It was such a beautiful and emotional moment. I was now Mrs. Sonia McLeod.

A few months after our wedding I started looking closely at my rings. What was amazing was that my promise ring had 15 small little diamonds in it, and my wedding band had five small diamonds in it! This was our wedding date: May 15, 2010. And those numbers, 5-15, have shown up everywhere we've gone. Our number is threaded through our lives. In fact, the promise of God we stand on for our marriage and ministry reflects this:

> And that he died for all, that they which live should not henceforth live unto themselves, but unto him which died for them, and rose again. (2 Corinthians 5:15)

We didn't stay in Cochrane for very long after we got married. Derek found a job in Prince George, British Columbia. We decided to launch out and move. It was a big move but we decided to go and it was the only place where he found a job. It was a brand-new start so we headed across Canada to BC. I didn't know this, but Derek had been given a promise from the Lord many years before. The Lord revealed to him that he would travel across Canada with his family. Neither of us had ever been that way before so it was going to be an adventure for us all for sure. It was a move by faith because we didn't know anyone out in B.C.

As we made our way west to BC we made a few stops. Our three young children Hassan, Kirsten, and Hasslina were with us as we hit the road. We were leaving behind family and friends and we knew it would be hard on all of us. After two days on the road from Cochrane, Ontario, we pulled into my mother's driveway in Yorkton, Saskatchewan. It was a welcome rest stop. We spent a few days with my mom before we headed off. Our next stop was in Red

Deer, Alberta. I had a good friend there who offered us a place to stay for the night. She and her husband had been my neighbors in Eckville, Alberta. They now lived in Red Deer. Our next stop was in Rocky Mountain House to visit Jean Stewart. Jean, and her late husband, Larry were the founders of Camp Living Water, a summer Bible camp for First Nation youth. These were stops with my friends whom I had met previously when I was in Alberta for a short time. I was excited to introduce them to my husband. They had been instrumental and a comfort to me at a time when my children and I had been abandoned by my ex-husband in Alberta a few years before. When we got to Rocky Mountain House, Jean told us about Pastor Larry Keegstra who ran the BC branch of Camp Living Water. She called him up and connected us with him. After prayer and hugs with Jean, we hit the road and went our way again.

Neither Derek nor I had ever been to British Columbia. It was absolutely breathtaking as we entered the Rocky Mountains. We travelled north through Banff and Jasper National Park toward Prince George. I drove the little Nissan while Derek drove the fully loaded 26' U-Haul truck. We worried that the U-Haul would not be able to make the journey up the mountains but thankfully it had enough power. And then as we entered the tops of the mountains it started snowing and it was somewhat nerve-wracking as we were quite high and the guardrails were the only thing that would have kept us on the road if we were to slip. But the Lord was with us and this was only the start of our journey together. I knew He had us in His hand.

Our first stop was near Vanderhoof BC, at Camp Living Water, which was managed and directed by Larry Keegstra. It was a camp for children from nearby First Nation reserves. And it was a nice camp. It was beside a beautiful lake. It had a big slide, the kind you went down on with a burlap potato sack. It was built as an outreach for First Nation children to tell them about Jesus Christ. We were fortunate that the camp was not in season because we got to stay in one of the cabins. It was a treat for all of us. It was our home until we found a place of our own in Prince George which was about an hour away.

After a couple of weeks we found a place in Prince George. It was a rough part of town and there was a lot of crime in that area but we didn't let it bother us. If it bothered Derek, he didn't say. I was comfortable with living in the hood but I knew it was different for my husband who had mostly lived in the bushland of Northern Ontario and Quebec. He grew up on the land and around the water, and he was from a small knit community. The house we found was nice! We had a big bathroom in our bedroom that came with a jacuzzi. I had my first island piece in the kitchen for cooking. It was a beautiful home. Then we started looking for a home church.

It was on our heart to begin a small outreach in Prince George. The need was great and we wanted to feed the people some hot food and share the Word of God. Derek and I looked around for a place to serve hot food with bannock. We found a church with a hall for rent and we made a call and left a message. We got a call back and went to see the hall. It was exactly what we were looking for. It had a kitchen and a place to hold gospel services. It was perfect for a small outreach.

We put up flyers and handed them out to people on the street. Derek made chili and I made the bannock. We held a short service and then we served chili and bannock. We saw the need in the city and we knew we had to serve the people. We handed Derek's testimony out on flyers. It was his testimony of how he went through depression and how the Lord kept him from the spirit of death and suicide that came with torment.

About a week later, as we held one of our outreaches, we sat down for chili and bannock and a man came to sit with us. He began talking to us and told Derek that he kept the testimony that we had handed out beside his bed at night and in his pocket during the day. He said that he also faced these same thoughts and the same suicide spirit as my husband did. He was extremely thankful for the testimony. It was the words of Christ that offered him hope and a good night's rest.

Our friend, Pastor Larry Keegstra, would often preach at a local street outreach in Prince George. It was here that I met a friend. She told us that there was a concert being held at the park downtown. We decided to go and when we got to the park there was already a lot of people there. As we walked through the park I heard the Lord ask me, "Would you still love me, if I didn't have more to give you?" I knew He would not remove his provision or His blessings from me, but I didn't know what it meant? But I answered Him, 'Yes I love you. I will always love you.' What I didn't know then was that my words would be tested through the years if I would continue to love Him despite what lay ahead.

Hassan was in high school and our daughters, Kirsten and Hasslina, were in middle school. Thankfully their schools were within walking distance. We gave the girls their first hamsters. The kids were all doing good. We had our first bout with head lice and that was an ordeal with two little girls. They both had long hair so that kept me busy for a couple weeks. My oldest son had a love for music. He was becoming an exceptional guitar player. He was a fine young man and I could see the Lord keeping him. Our girls were our jewels and they were adjusting to our new life in B.C.

But this would be the season that the spiritual battle my husband was in would become visible to me. On the surface everything in our lives appeared to be normal. The pictures that I posted on social media of our new home could never have suggested our real struggles. I didn't imagine that one day I would be writing about our lives. Who wants to talk about personal private matters? But I knew we weren't the only ones facing this kind of battle in our marriage. When we went out in public, I saw the expression of insecurities from other women who shared the same shame and anger. I recognized them because they mirrored my pain but they struggled in silence.

One day, as I came into our bedroom to sit on the edge of the bed to look out our window, I heard myself say "Teach me to war!" I was surprised by what came out of my mouth. It made me wonder what was coming our way.

Five

Facing Our Enemy

Summer 2010

The end of school arrived and the kids wanted to see their other parents in Ontario for their summer break. Derek was still new at the job and so he had to work. The plan was for me to take the kids back to Ontario with the vehicle and Derek would take the bus back and forth to work. It was hard for us both since we were newlyweds and I didn't want to go. The kids and I hit the road and we were gone for a couple of weeks. They all had a great time visiting, but we were all anxious to get home. My drive back to BC with the kids was a long one and one I won't soon forget. I was running on energy drinks cause I didn't get much sleep. I know that wasn't smart but it was a long two weeks for me. It was the first and last long trip I had to take alone with the kids. Derek was excited for us to get back. I know he missed me and I could hardly wait to see my husband.

When I got home he surprised me with a hot bath, a candy dish of M&M's, and candlelight. It was inviting and refreshing to jump in the tub and finally relax. He was romantic when he wanted to be.

When I finally got out of the bath my husband was laying in bed. I was ready to sleep but before I shut the lights off and jumped in bed with him, I saw what appeared to me to be shadows of other people in bed with him. It freaked me right out but I passed it off as being tired. I would know later down the road that it was in fact something spiritual in our home. What I didn't know was that while I was away my husband had been consuming porn.

We had been looking for a church to attend and we had decided to visit a particular one that coming Sunday morning. We dressed up and headed out. That Sunday morning was going to be a service that I would not soon forget. I didn't know that my eyes would be opened to the spiritual war my husband was in.

After the worship service a woman wearing a white sheer blouse went to the front to talk about a book, *"Crazy Love"* by Francis Chan that she had just finished reading. As she was talking, I began to see images – sexual images – that came to life. The scene played out in front of me like an R-rated movie. I saw the outline of her breasts through her shirt and could see her blouse open up suddenly. It was very uncomfortable and I looked over to my husband and his eyes were glued to the front, like a deer caught in headlights. I knew that my husband was becoming aroused from watching her. I was becoming sick watching him knowing what was happening. When we got home, we went to our bedroom and after describing what I had seen at church, I asked him if that's what he saw. And he confirmed what I had seen. I was hoping that he would have told me 'No' and that it was just something crazy that had happened in my own mind. I lost it on him and started yelling. The pornographic images that he had consumed and had fed his lust throughout the years would now feed on and visually molest any woman who happened to be nearby. I felt hurt and betrayed.

Why did I have to see or know about it at all? I didn't understand.

But this unseen enemy had now shown itself and it was determined to destroy our marriage.

We took a drive through downtown Prince George one afternoon. My heart was heavy with everything that my eyes had been opened up to see. The enemy that taunted me was much bigger than I had imagined. Our marriage was not off to a good start. It was then that the Lord spoke to me about keeping my eyes on Him and not what I saw. My prayers were ineffective if I kept my eyes on the things around me. I had to keep my eyes up above on Him, and not down here. I had to submit to the Lord and get out of His way and learn how to fully surrender my husband over to Him. The hardest part was letting go and trusting the Lord with it all. I was hindering what Jesus wanted to do in my heart by being angry. There were parts of my heart that the Lord wanted me to surrender and to be completely yielded. The heart is deep and who can know it?

We would both come to learn that there is no height or depth to His love. He went to the cross and died for people. Would I carry my cross and follow Him? Would I obey Him and do what He asked of me? It would be a long process, but I would yield and obey. It would cut and wound my heart, but I would see the fruit by my obedience.

The fights and arguments we had in the beginning of our marriage were the toughest. They say that the first three years of marriage are the hardest. It didn't look like we would survive the first year after we had a major blow up one day. We got into an argument and he stormed out of the house with our briefcase that held our documents and money. I followed his trail yelling behind him. We were arguing on one of the main highways in Prince George. When I caught up to him, I tried grabbing the briefcase from him, but my husband is a giant compared to me so I was no match for him. He yanked it away and stomped off again. So if anyone remembers seeing two crazy people fighting over a briefcase on the side of the road? That was us.

On another intense night of arguing, I jumped in the vehicle and planned to leave him and drive to Saskatchewan. But while I was on my way, a snowstorm rose up out of nowhere and I could barely see the road in front of me. With treacherous mountain roads in front of me that would no doubt be closed, I had no choice but to turn around and go home. As I headed back home, I knew it was the Lord's doing for turning me around. The move to Prince George BC was proving to be necessary for us both. It is no wonder the Lord told me to keep my eyes on him. He was looking for me to run to Him so He could show himself strong if I could yield to Him. But I was fighting for control in this situation. I was being ruled by my emotions and by what I saw. We both needed to grow up and mature in our faith. I would come to understand the sexual bondage my husband struggled with and I had to learn how to give up control.

2010

British Columbia is a beautiful province. At least that's what we thought until we found out about the "Highway of Tears." It is actually named after two highways which intersect in the city. On these two highways, many Indigenous women have gone missing or have been found murdered while hitchhiking. The area that once felt beautiful and green was now eerie and dark. It reminded me of the story of Cain and Abel in the Bible. The book of Genesis tells how Cain killed his brother Abel and the blood of Abel cried out to God. That's what I felt the spilled blood on the land around us was doing. It was calling out for justice. Justice for the blood of our Indigenous people. Our native women were being raped, murdered, and tossed out like garbage.

As Derek and I were driving back from Walmart one afternoon, we saw a native woman who was hitchhiking. I suggested we turn around to pick her up and take her where she wanted to go. I couldn't stand the thought of anything happening to her when we could have done something to prevent it. He turned around and we went and picked her up. When we pulled over she jumped in and she seemed relieved that she saw an Indigenous couple. We could tell though that she was still quite nervous. My heart went out to her because hitchhiking was her means of transportation. We took her home which was several miles out of town. I asked her if there were buses or any other means to travel. She told me she had no vehicle, and that others had to hitchhike into town to do their shopping or just to get off the reservation. There isn't much to do on the reservation. There isn't much for employment. Alcohol and drug addiction rates are high. She told us how she was nervous and knew she was risking her life each time she jumped into a vehicle. At least we were able to help her get home. But we knew there were many before and after her that would go missing.

Derek went on a 21-day fast and he was believing for deliverance. It was during that fast that the Lord spoke to Derek that we were going to have a son and we were to call him David. Well, Derek had three daughters already and I doubted at times that we would have a son. I didn't share my doubts with him because I wanted to believe him, but I wondered about it. Although I was 37 years old I was not concerned about my age. Then it happened, I got pregnant. Derek started to suspect that I was because I couldn't watch a movie without falling asleep. I would be sleeping within 20 minutes of watching one. Then I started waking up feeling nauseous in the mornings and I had to know if I was pregnant.

One morning, after Derek went to work, I walked to the dollar store for a pregnancy test. What would the accuracy be on a cheap brand? But the test came back with a positive result. Now, I couldn't wait for Derek to get back because I needed to go and buy a brand name one that cost me double because I didn't trust the dollar store brand. When he got home, we left right away and the test was a positive one. We were having a baby! I was overjoyed and we were both excited. It had been a long time since I had a baby in the house. My oldest son was in high school. Both of our youngest girls were nine years old. We sat the kids down at the kitchen table and told them that we were going to have a baby. They were incredibly happy to hear they were going to have a little brother or sister. It was a shock to them though. Since my last pregnancy was more than ten years before, it took a toll on my body this time. I was exhausted. And with the news of expecting a baby, we decided to head back to Ontario. We wanted to be closer to our family and friends. We packed up and hit the road. We were moving back to Cochrane where we first met and got married.

PART TWO

I Will Have Mercy

But I will have mercy upon the house of Judah,
and will save them by the Lord their God, and will not save them by
bow, nor by sword, nor by battle, by horses, nor by horsemen.
Hosea 1:7

Six

A Coming Time of Sifting

Back to Cochrane

The Lord will use all things for our good and for His glory. He reminded me of this when we moved back to Cochrane, Ontario, from British Columbia.

We had rented a U-Haul once again. As we did on our way out to BC, we stopped at my mom's in Yorkton. The new year was just a couple days away. Derek had to travel a day ahead because of the rental agreement return date for the truck. I would be driving with the kids. We were hoping that I would get to Cochrane by New Year's Eve so that we could all be together. I had planned to leave the next morning, but Hasslina started to complain about her ear that night. I found this quite strange because Hasslina never had any earaches as a child.

The drive through Manitoba was uneventful and everyone was glad to be headed back to Ontario. As we entered Ontario, it was now dark and everything was closed, except for gas stations. Hasslina had been pretty quiet for most of the drive, but now she was experiencing pain in her ear. Thunder Bay was still a drive away so we decided to stop in Kenora.

When we woke up the following morning there was blood coming from her ear. I was freaked out. She never got earaches and this was definitely worrisome. I called Derek and told him that I was going to take Hasslina to the nearest hospital along the way. He told me that would be in Dryden which was less than two hours away. It was mild and snowing as we drove into Dryden and to the hospital. Once there she was seen almost immediately. We found out she had a perforated eardrum. She was treated and right afterward we hit the road again. About an hour or so later, we encountered a police roadblock. I pulled up and the officer told me that they had just shut the road down and that it wouldn't be opening for quite a while. They said that semi-trailer trucks had gone off the road. He said that the highway was like a skating rink! We couldn't go any further. We would have to stay a night in a nearby motel.

I called Derek to let him know what had happened. We both knew that God had allowed this to happen with Hasslina's ear, otherwise we would have kept going and had we been maybe just 20 – 30 minutes earlier, we would have been on that road. We likely could have been involved with one of those semi-trailers.

This whole episode really ministered to my heart that sometimes the delays we face is oftentimes the Lord protecting us. He used a broken eardrum to delay our trip and keep from us entering that dangerous section of highway. What's even more remarkable is that not only did He protect us from harm, but also Hasslina's ear was healed, and she hasn't experienced another earache since!

We found a decent little house in Cochrane and even got our first dog! This was a big step for Derek. He never wanted an animal in our house so something was slowly changing in him.

I was getting bigger now and we decided to get a 3D ultrasound to see our baby. We wanted to know if we were having a boy or a girl. We had to drive to Sudbury, Ontario which meant a day of travel. Derek rented a room for us in a small town near Sudbury. We stayed the night there before waking up the next morning to drive to Sudbury for our appointment.

The day we headed to Sudbury for the ultrasound will always be remembered because it was on March 11, 2011. It was the same day a tsunami hit Japan and over 10,000 lives were lost. The world watched as the water rushed in and flattened homes and took lives. On our day of joy, halfway around the world there were cries of sorrow. As we drove toward our destination, a bad snowstorm hit the area and we had no choice but to take a chance to navigate through the storm. We knew we wouldn't cancel for anything. We had to confirm if we were going to have a little girl, or a little boy. We made it in time for the appointment, although we had hoped to have something to eat when we arrived. The storm had slowed us down considerably.

The technician called us into the room and I laid down on the table. They put the jelly lubricant on my belly and she began scanning. We watched as this little life moved around inside me. I noticed that the heartbeat was nice and strong. She kept moving the instrument around on my belly. We both waited anxiously to hear what she would say. After what seemed like an eternity, she turned to us and said, "You're having a boy." I looked over at my husband and could see complete joy on his face. I knew he was amazed to see that what he had been believing was now confirmed. If he had his doubts about a boy he never voiced it to me. We didn't talk about it but we both anticipated this day to come. David McLeod was on his way.

I don't remember having many food cravings but my checkups were going well. I started having gallbladder attacks and I didn't gain much weight. I had to visit the hospital emergency room a few times in extreme pain for the attacks, but I had no other problems with my pregnancy. I was thankful to the Lord that despite the gall-bladder attacks, no harm came to my baby.

On April 27, 2011, we learned that Rev. David Wilkerson had passed away in a car accident. That was devastating to me and I was shocked. I had gleaned so much from his ministry that I felt he had been like a spiritual father to me and it was hard to believe that he was gone. I knew that a genuine man of God had left us and there were only a few like him. He was truly an authentic man of God who loved Jesus like no other person I knew. Our son's name, David, now had so much more meaning to me. I don't know if that was the reason why the Lord gave us the name for our son, but we were thankful He had.

I loved being pregnant and found it miraculous and amazing to carry a life inside my womb. I carried him full term and delivered him at Timmins Hospital. He was born healthy and was absolutely perfect including his cone shaped head he had when he was born. He was adorable. Things could have gone differently if it wasn't for the Lord keeping him. When it was time for delivery the obstetrician didn't come. It was the nurse who delivered him. David had been in the birthing canal longer than he should have. The attending nurse didn't know why my heart rate was going up and down, or why his heart rate kept dropping. It started to cause us concern and she would have me flip from one side to the other. When the time came it was the nurse who delivered my baby. The whole experience we had at the hospital was not a good one. We were thankful to the Lord that David was born healthy and we could go home. He would be my last baby born at the hospital.

Another Woman, Another Incident

One day, we went to a fair that was being held in Timmins. We often went there when we had to go to Walmart or to do our bigger shopping. But we wanted to go to the fair. And at any fair they have rides, good food and lots of people. It wouldn't take long when we got there that Derek noticed another woman to stare at and it wounded me. I was embarrassed by it and ashamed because I always knew when something was exchanged between him and someone else. The other woman would always look back at me. I never knew what she would be thinking, but I sure felt as though I had the word "fool" written on my forehead. We headed home and we started arguing. At one point, he pulled over and got out of the vehicle, and started walking away from me. I ran after him and tried to talk to him to get into the vehicle to go home. He wasn't listening to me. I knew when he got to this point there was no talking to him, he defended his position and couldn't admit to me or see the hurt he was doing to me. He always turned it on me that everything was somehow my fault. I went back to the vehicle and drove alongside him but he wasn't budging. So there we were, Derek walking on the side of the road in a huff and miles away from home. We were around bushes and the only thing around us were quite possibly bears or wolves. He wouldn't come with me no matter how much I pleaded and he told me he was going to walk home. I wasn't going to try anymore and so I left.

I took the kids back home and went back for him. I was nervous and scared though. From when he started walking to when I got back to him was about three or so hours. It was starting to get dark. Would I find him? And as I came around a bend, there he was. When I got to him he jumped right in. The only ones that had stopped for him were the police. They carded him since he was walking down a highway by himself. I guess they wanted to make sure he wasn't an escaped convict or wanted for any reason.

The ride back was silent, but along the way home, he told me that the Lord convicted his heart. He knew that the Lord had spoken to him while he was walking. He felt that the Lord told him that things were going to be hard, the journey would hurt at times, but if he wanted to make it home he needed to keep putting one foot in front of the other – no matter how much it hurt. This would become something we would always look back on how the Lord spoke to Derek. It's something we still say today to encourage one another, "Just keep putting one foot in front of the other."

Ordained – May 2011

After moving back to Cochrane we decided to attend church at the local First Nations church. Derek knew the pastor and we both helped out in services with music and sharing the Word. Soon the pastor told us that he wanted us to get ordained at the upcoming assembly of the Independent Assemblies. It also happened to be the same assembly that Derek's father would be getting ordained at too. We traveled down and met them there.

I wanted it to be a beautiful day, but I can still vividly recall the hurt I felt on that day. The spirit of lust was present and it was all over my husband. He was not ready to be ordained. He just couldn't see how blind he was to everything at that point. He was so bound in this lustful religious spirit that he thought he was good the way he was. We stood there before the service began, and I was crying and hurting inside. And the only thing on my mind was how my husband was a fraud and a phony. That's how I felt because I had never witnessed him in a real intimate relationship with Jesus Christ. Yet, we were both ordained that day.

As we left London, I drove with my mother-in-law and my husband drove with his dad. This has always been a bittersweet and laughable moment. I had a moment with my mother-in-law that we still laugh about today. We entered Toronto down the 401, Canada's busiest stretch of highway. I had grown up in large urban areas and so it was nothing for me to weave in and out of traffic. I asked my mother-in-law if she could see where my husband was. He was behind me and I needed to know if we were supposed to take an exit off the freeway. I couldn't understand why she was so quiet and barely talked to me. I found out later that the reason she didn't say anything was because she was terrified. She was from the North and she wasn't used to the freeway – at least not to my driving and to being in a small car in the middle of rush hour traffic in Canada's largest city. I gave it no thought and just thought she was being quiet. But that was not the case at all. That story is something we still laugh at today. It was a funny and cherished moment in the midst of a bitter time. It was a time when my husband was so blind to his sin.

Brantford, ON

Derek's work in Cochrane was coming to an end. We headed down south for another job. This time we were moving to southern Ontario. The move down was rough because we lost the air conditioning in the car. The closer we got to the south, it got more humid and much hotter. A huge traffic jam made it worse and we had to put David in the cab of the U-Haul to keep him cool and from overheating in the car.

We were heading to Brantford, Ontario near the Six Nations reserve. Derek had found another contract. The jobs he found that fit his experience were often contracts that lasted only a year. Then he would need to find another job when the year was done. He was good at administration work and also did some graphic design. He had always wanted to become a pilot so he looked around in the area for aviation training. We were happy when he found one so he started his ground school training. I was afraid of heights but I knew when the time came I would be there for him when he became a pilot. It didn't take him long before he was doing his flight training and he was able to take David and I up with him. I climbed up on that small plane that day fully trusting this metal machinery to keep us alive. I was praying the whole time we were up there. The turbulence made me sick to my stomach but it was the experience of a lifetime to watch my hubby flying an aircraft. David was asleep in his car seat the whole time. I was grateful that he wasn't crying or scared.

It wasn't long before I started to show signs that I could be pregnant again. I was feeling nauseous and tired. The belief I had that you can't get pregnant while nursing went out the door. I still had the extra pregnancy test that came with the first pregnancy pack I bought when I had David. I ran to go look for it in my bathroom drawer and found it. I did the test and left it on the bathroom counter and ran down to change my laundry. When I came back a few minutes later and checked, it was showing a positive result. I called out, "DERRREK!" He came running as quick as he could and saw the positive result of another pregnancy test. And he said "NOOO WAY!" But we were happy to get pregnant again. David was only a few weeks old by this time. I remember my mother saying to me that we would be popping them out after we got married. I loved children but with all the gallbladder attacks I was having I knew I needed to have my gallbladder removed. I had hoped to have the operation done before I got pregnant again. It was too late for that now. Ready or not, we were having another baby. I was still nursing David. But this time we decided to have a home birth.

We did some research and found a First Nation Birthing Center on Six Nations. We called and set up an appointment. We met our midwives and preparations were made and set to have our baby at home. I had wondered about home births before and the thought of having a baby without an epidural didn't appeal to me. But it turned out to be the best decision we could have made. We had the best midwives to deliver our son Joshua. This was by far the best experience that we both had and Derek was with me every step of the way. Although in the beginning we were not so sure about one of our midwives. She moved slowly and that concerned us a bit. We wondered if we could feel confident with her when the time came for Joshua to be born. Another midwife seemed to have our trust much more than she did. But when it came time to deliver our son, the one we did not fully trust was the swiftest and most assured. She sprang into action with confidence and put us all at ease.

We had two midwives and one of them showed Derek how to hold my hips when contractions came. He was to hold them firmly until the contractions passed. This helped a lot to ease my pain. When he didn't hold my hips in place the pain was unbearable. And when it got to the point where I thought I was going to literally die and needed to go to the hospital, the midwife who we thought was too slow, said that was usually the time to give birth. She stated that when mom begins to feel that way then baby was ready to come. She ordered me to get up on the bed because she had to check how far I was dilated. In my mind I thought she was crazy! Getting up on the bed seemed like mission impossible. The next contraction was coming and there was nothing I could do about it, so I climbed up on the bed. But she was right, it wasn't long after that when I was told to push!

The midwives directed Derek to get into position so that he could catch Joshua. It didn't take long and, with one final push, Joshua came out and he almost slipped out of daddy's hands. The midwives and Derek all exclaimed, 'Whoa!' But daddy caught him and it was a beautiful moment. Joshua was perfect and the miracle of life still amazes me. Our daughter Kirsten said when she went to the bathroom that morning she heard his first cry. She was stunned and surprised. The experience of a home birth was incredible and the midwives stayed and watched the boys while we caught up on some sleep. We slept while the midwives took care of things for us at home.

We had two amazing sons eleven months apart. Their oldest siblings adored them. I stopped nursing David and started nursing

Joshua. It was hard on me emotionally that my baby wasn't my baby for very long before I had all my attention on the other one. David had to get used to sleeping in the crib in his own room. I can remember crying with him at times outside his door while he was weaning and learning to sleep by himself. We were doing well and Daddy was right there to help out when I needed him. One night when I got up to nurse Joshua, and while nursing, I fell asleep, and he fell to the floor. We were sleeping on a mattress on the floor so he didn't fall far. Derek woke up and asked what happened. I said, "Nothing!" while grabbing him as quickly as I could off the floor! He was good and didn't cry. Daddy changed diapers and held them when I needed rest. It wasn't long before they were sitting up and crawling around. They were the cutest little rascals ever.

Soon after, my husband's battle would come to the surface again. I guess it was always there but I was busy with being a mom again and looking after our family.

I was beginning to notice him looking at other women. One could say that it was hardly a struggle for him, but enjoyment. And I'm sure it was exciting for him with the sexual images he entertained but it always came at a cost and left him beaten down and in turmoil.

We are no match over the powers of darkness on our own. We don't realize how controlled and enslaved we are until we try to walk away from it. And we are powerless to change until we're fully surrendered to the Lord. He has to be Lord over our life.

Pornography is like a drug and once it owns you, you become enslaved to it. The images that consume the mind in private will parade around when you're out with your family. It's there to seduce you until it takes control.

We liked to take long drives and this was something we enjoyed doing while listening to a sermon. We enjoyed our drives even more now that it helped to put our boys to sleep when they needed a nap.

They would be sleeping in a few minutes in the vehicle. We needed gas so we drove to the gas station on Six Nation's reserve. I was in the back seat with Joshua. It was easier to sit next to him if he needed to nurse. I noticed a vehicle pull up in front of our vehicle. My heart sank and my body began shaking as I watched from the back seat Derek and the girl in the next vehicle stare at each other. It was a full-service gas station. Her partner went into the store and she was waiting for him while both her and Derek were having a moment together. I could tell by the way he was staring at her that he had only her in his mind. And there I was in the back holding our one-month-old baby. I don't remember what I said but I interrupted that real quick. I wanted to slap him upside the head because he was making a fool out of me. I was angry and hurt. She didn't know I was sitting in the back seat and I couldn't blame her. Then her boyfriend/husband came back after getting the gas and as they were driving away, I watched her staring back at him. I felt complete betrayal. It was at these moments when I questioned everything and wondered if things would ever change.

Yorkton, Saskatchewan

It wasn't long before Derek's contract for work came to an end and we had to think about moving again. I was looking forward to leaving this time because this area brought a lot of pain for me. The agency he worked for didn't renew the project and his contract was not renewed as well. I called my mom and told her about what was happening and she suggested we come to Saskatchewan. My uncle also suggested coming because there was lots of work out that way. We had very little other choice so we headed to Saskatchewan. We stayed with my mom in her basement until we got a place of our own.

Although it wasn't where I wanted to be because of past hurts, I was back in the province of Saskatchewan. Despite this, I decided I was going to love my family. My family is very involved in ministry. I have two aunts who, along with their husbands, pastor churches in Saskatchewan. One of them was hosting special services where my father was going to be their special speaker. We decided that we would show our love and support by going to their church and attending their special services. I was going to trust the Lord for restoration between them and myself. We decided to go and although it was awkward, we had a good time.

On our way home, which was about an hour drive, Derek, suddenly and unexpectedly, told me that the Lord was going to anoint me in the midst of my family who had rejected me. He spoke of the story of David in Samuel 16 when the prophet Samuel was directed by God to anoint David as king of Israel. David's father, Jesse, was asked by Samuel to call for his sons because God had chosen one of them to be king. Jesse brought all his children before Samuel, except one – David. He had been overlooked. The Lord refused all of Jesse's sons and this caused Samuel to ask Jesse if all his sons were there. It was only then that Jesse called for David. When David was brought in, Samuel immediately heard the Lord speak to him that this was the one God had chosen. In the midst of all his family, David was anointed king. It wasn't David's stature or looks that God was seeking, it was his heart.

I knew it was a word from the Lord. When Derek told me this story, I sensed the presence of God upon me. I knew He would do it. It did surprise me because I didn't understand how it was going to happen.

Although the Lord would use him throughout our marriage to speak to me, Derek's wandering eyes continued and I became more bitter. I continued to pray and trust the Lord with it all.

I was doing interviews for my book, *Rise Up My Beloved*. The book was still moving and it was changing lives. This was encouraging because I needed it. I would pray to hear a report from someone who read it and every time without fail, I would receive one. I had to trust the Lord despite what was happening in our marriage. We walked by faith and not by sight. We didn't trust our emotions to lead us but we moved by His Word and walked by it. The Lord has everything in His hands and why should we worry? The book was moving and those who read it always said they couldn't put the book down. The Lord had changed my life miraculously and, despite the fiery trials we seemed to be walking through, He hadn't just suddenly stopped moving in my life.

We couldn't find a place to live in Yorkton at this time so we had to look for other options. We had applied for a house on Cowessess and got one. We moved out to Cowessess First Nation reserve, about an hour outside of Yorkton. It worked out for us because Derek's job was in Cowessess and he had been commuting there every day.

A couple of months later a subsidized house became available for us in Yorkton. It was a nice town and it wasn't too big but perfect for raising a family. It offered many opportunities for recreational sports and activities. I had a close uncle on my mother's side that lived in Yorkton. And my home reservation was close by and within driving distance. Derek commuted back and forth to work on Cowessess until he found another job in Yorkton.

As I was driving home one evening, the Lord brought to my mind the story of the woman's baby who died in the night and switched her dead baby with another woman's baby (1 King 3:16-38). When the woman woke up she knew her baby had been switched. She knew that the dead baby wasn't hers and because they could not resolve this they went to king Solomon. The woman who woke up with the dead baby told the king that the other woman had switched the babies and had put the dead baby beside her. The women continued arguing back and forth and the woman who switched the baby wouldn't tell the truth. The king then made the judgment to cut the baby in half and give each half of the baby to each woman.

But the real mother cried out and said, give her the baby! King Solomon knew who the real mother was because he knew that the real mother would not want her baby to be cut in half. Why was He showing me this? The answer to my question would soon come.

I loved my daughters and I understood that these children were gifts to me from the Lord. I would be held accountable for all of them. I had to love and nurture all those He placed in my hands. We were a blended family, could it be hard to love and rear another woman's baby and love them as my own? Could I do it?

Our daughters were doing good but the time came when my stepdaughter and my daughter started drifting apart. In school my stepdaughter Kirsten excelled academically and she thrived in everything she did. And my daughter began to struggle academically and it was hard to watch. I began to resent my stepdaughter. I had to surrender the hurt over to the Lord because I knew that all my children were gifts to me. I was entrusted with his daughters and they were mine now too. My husband encouraged me one day and said he heard wisdom when Hasslina talked about different things and it wasn't anything specific but the Lord was showing him things about her. Wisdom came from the Lord. And He had her in His hands despite her struggles.

When we moved into our place in Yorkton, Derek wanted to paint the living room. I had no problem with that, I figured since he did graphic designing that he could probably do a good job with the decor. He painted the walls green and to this day it is our reminder that I do the interior decor. We still laugh at that wall because it was such a shiny green and it was a definite eyesore. I was still putting my Bible scriptures up in the house but not to the extreme of painting "Jesus Lives" in red bold cursive on my wall. This was something I had done previously as a single parent. It was my signature wall. I knew people thought I was a little extreme with my Jesus and my

Bible verses. I wasn't sure how Derek would take to my art being on the wall.

One evening on one of our usual drives on the outskirts of Yorkton, we experienced a "heaven moment" with the Lord. We don't remember the discussion we were having but we can both recall a very real presence of the Lord with us in the vehicle. It was as if He were physically sitting with us as we were driving. And the Word we both heard was that Satan desired to sift us as wheat (Luke 22:31-32). We knew that our faith in God would be tested somehow. We would be stretched and would have to face the fire, but the Lord Jesus was there praying for us that we would endure. This moment would come back to us in our time of great testing.

We found a local church in Yorkton and I was looking forward to the fellowship and meeting new people. One would think church would be the safest place to be and that people would be there to hear a word from the Lord. A word that would change their lives but it would not be the place to go and blatantly sin. Church wasn't supposed to be a pick-up place, or a singles club. But it was beginning to feel like that and could sense that this is what some churches have come to. It was during praise and worship that I noticed my husband and the woman at the front who was singing, staring at one another. I felt anger and shame. I wanted to go up and say something to the woman who couldn't take her eyes off my husband. I was livid and felt more and more like a fool and embarrassed about my hubby's behavior because my husband couldn't keep himself under control!

We got into an argument one afternoon and I told him to leave, just get out! If he wanted to be busy looking elsewhere he was free to do it. He left and he was gone for several days. I was bothered by how distant he was with me. He sent me an email about child support and lawyers. I sent it to a friend because I was shocked by his response to me. She said that he was cold. There was a coldness to him that I hadn't seen before. It was during this time of separation that the Lord spoke to me about holding on to my marriage. He showed me an image of me sitting in a boat with several other smaller boats around me. I knew those who were sitting in the boats were watching my life. I could not just do what I wanted in my life without there being any repercussions of my actions. My life was no longer mine but it belonged to the Lord. The Lord confirmed this when I called a sister in the Lord later that evening.

I was sharing with her how discouraged I was feeling and I felt like giving up on our marriage. She told me that if I gave up others would too. She recalled a sermon by David Wilkerson and it's probably one I had heard too at some point because he had been like a spiritual father to me. She went on to say that she sees me in a boat and there were other smaller boats around me and they were watching me. This life was not my own. I had to press through for the Lord and press through for my marriage. I promised myself that I would never kick him out again. I didn't want to lose my marriage. I had to fight for it. I wasn't naïve and knew that things were not going to be easy.

We have a very real enemy who wants to destroy us and our children. And his target is our family. If he brings us down, he can consume our children. He is relentless and his time upon earth is short.

But before things got worse, we managed to talk and I told him I would never kick him out again. He had told me the reason for his coldness was because he felt like I was rejecting him. He didn't want to feel that by me and I knew that there was a deep root of rejection in his heart. I had to continue to love him and do what the Lord asked me to do and put him in His hands. I could not change him. That was not my job to do; it was the work of the Holy Spirit that would change him. But what I needed to do was to love him.

I knew my husband loved me. I knew he knew the word of God. I would always be asking myself, 'why can't he fight for us through prayer?' I knew he had a hard time praying, but how hard could that be if he really loved me? I couldn't talk to anyone because my husband sang and did worship ministry. He was anointed to sing. I honored my husband and wanted to protect him and not shame him in any way. He could preach the word powerfully at times and other times, he struggled. I knew the anointing of the Lord was upon his life hence the battle he was under. I asked him one day about the New Covenant and if he understood what it meant. Did he know of the promises of God and did he know who he was in Christ? I knew he knew the Word and he could tell me more of the Word than I could. When I would question him he would get upset and defensive. He didn't like to be made to feel guilty or feel the need to examine himself. I would feel like I was tip-toeing on egg-shells all the time. I had to be careful how I said things around him. I struggled in silence but continued to cry out to the Lord. Every time I caught him watching other women it hurt. I felt that I wasn't sexually appealing for my husband. I wasn't "sexy" enough and he wasn't attracted to me anymore. The Lord was working in my heart. He was digging deeper into the recesses of it and I had to get out of God's way. We were contending with enemies far greater than ourselves.

Called Back to Ontario

We received a call from the Chief of Derek's community. This was where Derek had grown up. He was calling to ask Derek for help in dealing with the community's legal challenge and land claims. He was putting a team together and asked Derek to lead the communications part of the team. We weren't ready to move up to Moose Factory and housing was unavailable. Derek asked if he could work from a remote location, but yet near enough to travel there as needed. The Chief agreed to this and that's what we did. I wanted to go to school and Derek did most of his work online. We decided to go to North Bay, ON because it was the perfect spot that worked for us all. It was situated nicely where the kids could visit their other parents and Derek could travel for work. For me, London was only a five-hour drive from North Bay.

I liked North Bay but it was cold in the winter. It was a dry cold and come wintertime you needed a parka to live there. The town was by a lake called Lake Nipissing and the beach was beautiful in the summertime. This was the first time I learned of the shad fly. They are bugs and are known to that part of the North. I was told that their plentiful presence was a sign of a healthy ecosystem, but I didn't care, they did not look friendly and I didn't like them. Our son got a job at Pizza Pizza down by the waterfront. One night he sent me a picture. The front door of the restaurant was covered in shad flies. They didn't bite and we had nothing to worry about except for the fact that they were gross looking. They only came for a few weeks and then they disappeared.

North Bay has a large population of First Nation people, and like any other place with a bigger native population, there are a lot of substance abuse problems. We knew we wanted to have an outreach to feed and minister to our First Nation people in the area. We found a small street front space and everything came together. There were a few regular people that came out but looking back at that time now, we were obviously not ready to pastor.

My husband had a desire to do the work of the ministry, but he did not have a burden for the lost. Although he would have said he did he just didn't like people back then. And his heart was still carrying a lot of hurt. As long as he was doing the "work" of ministry he thought he was doing good. No matter how "good" his "works" may have been, the spirits of religion and lust would always rear their ugly heads in his life. And after they did, he would then fall under heavy condemnation.

My husband and I went for a walk one evening because it was

such a beautiful evening. And along our way, we came across a young First Nation man. After we talked with him for a few minutes, and invited him out to our outreach, I suddenly got very uncomfortable. I had been wearing a light summer dress, and every time the wind would pick up, his eyes would follow my dress. I could see that he was struggling with lust and was having a very difficult time talking with us. His eyes couldn't stop looking at my dress. I felt compassion upon him. He was alone and was homeless. He needed a touch from the Lord and He was his only hope. So many men struggle and are enslaved by this demonic spirit of lust. Many are without the Lord, and although some find the Lord, they continue to struggle with this enemy. My husband was one of the latter.

There have been countless times through the years that I have asked the Lord to show me that His hand was on my husband. The battle would get hard sometimes and I needed to see the Lord move through him. In between his highs and lows, I prayed for the Lord to speak to and through my husband. And He was always faithful.

One night in particular as he was playing his guitar, he suddenly told me that he had to go upstairs and write a song. He went upstairs for about half an hour and then came back downstairs. He started singing the most beautiful song I had ever heard in my life. It brought me to tears and the Lord's hand was all over it. The lyrics spoke of a time when I lived as an addict on the street. I was high as could be, wanting to die, but the Lord saw me and He kept His hand on me. While I was on those streets, Jesus saw me. Derek entitled the song *Little Indian Girl*. If you would like to hear the song you can find it on our YouTube channel.

Seven

Let Christ's Light Shine

I wanted to go back to school. It was also at this time I wanted to learn more about Fetal Alcohol Spectrum Disorder (FASD). We found out that a local First Nation private college had a course that interested me. I applied to Anishinabek Educational Institute (AEI) for the FASD course. My reservation would not help me with the cost of the program but one of the school counsellors that I had spoken to about enrolling into the program said they would look into something and get back to me. She called me back and told me that the total cost of the program would be covered!

Anishinabek Educational Institute took great pride in their native ceremonial traditions and teachings. I was aware of that before I started attending classes, but it was a chance for me to be a light while I was there. In class one day, we sat and had a discussion. Someone asked, "How do we deal with pain?" I shared how Jesus Christ changed my life and how He healed my heart. What I found amazing was that they listened. I knew that a few of my colleagues didn't share my beliefs but I did not let that bother me. I studied hard and completed my assignments while raising our two growing little boys. Whenever I had opportunity in class I spoke of Jesus Christ. At the end of the year I got the shocking news that I was chosen to be valedictorian. Only the Lord could have done that. I was given the honor to proclaim the name of Jesus in a native college centered on culture and ceremonies.

It was 2016 and our our lives were about to be completely changed.

Our daughters would both be celebrating their sweet sixteen birthdays. It was supposed to be a year of celebration. But it was not to be. Hasslina had been complaining often of headaches. We didn't think much of it and passed it off as just needing more water. One evening, I went to her room and I could see that she wasn't feeling well. She told me her head was hurting and spinning, she could barely walk. Over the next few weeks we took several trips to the ER and each time she was sent home with no resolution or diagnosis. There was one time that she was so sick and so pale that I truly thought I was going to lose her. Despite these scary moments, she had a pediatrician who didn't think there was much to be concerned about.

Soon she started complaining that she was always seeing flashing lights in her peripheral vision. I decided to take her to the eye doctor. I knew he suspected something more serious was going on with her health. He immediately wrote up a referral to her doctor to be seen by a specialist. Finally, her doctor scheduled an MRI for her. When the results came back the doctor called us to her office. No one could have prepared me for the news that would come.

We sat across from the doctor as she opened her computer. She looked at her screen and then turned to me and said, "Hasslina has Multiple Sclerosis." I didn't know what to say. I knew I couldn't fall apart because Hasslina was seated next to me. This doctor had not been very warm, nor friendly, but aloof. And I was upset with her for not asking me to make sure I came with my husband or have support in place when she delivered this devastating news. I knew MS wasn't a death sentence and although I didn't know entirely what MS was, I knew it wasn't good. It was just two weeks before her sixteenth birthday!

A quick Google search and we learned that MS is an auto-immune disease that attacks the myelin sheath. The myelin sheath is important because it protects the neurons in the brain. MS attacks the myelin sheath which ultimately causes irreparable damage to the neurological system. As it progresses, the long-term outcome can be debilitating. We were referred to an MS specialist. Soon after, she started daily injections which she had to administer herself.

In the days and weeks following, I cried and couldn't stop crying. Why? Why Lord? Why my daughter? And the story about the two women who went to King Solomon for help came back to me. It felt like my daughter was dying and would it cause me to be bitter? My heart hurt so much. She had so much happening in her life, and to be diagnosed with MS at 15 years old was rare. People were usually diagnosed with this much later in life. My heart broke into a million pieces. At night I would sob uncontrollably at times for my only daughter. What calmed my heart was watching Hasslina walk through this like it was nothing. If she had fears or if she was scared she never voiced it. Hasslina had always been one to hate any kind of needles. I was shocked at how she was able to give the injections to herself. But here she was giving herself these injections. I knew that the Lord was with us, and with her. We held on to His Word that this was not unto death but for the glory of His name.

When Jesus heard that, he said, This sickness is not unto death, but for the glory of God, that the Son of God might be glorified thereby. (John 11:4)

I had to believe that through this dark time the Lord was doing a deep work in her heart and in mine. He was doing something far greater than I could understand. I knew that He loved her and He had a perfect plan for her life. Hasslina was special from birth. She had been born with six toes. When she was two years old she had to go for surgery to remove her little toes on each foot. I remember how frightened I was and thinking that something could go wrong in the surgery room. I'll always remember the Lord comforting my heart that day, and saying to me to thank Him for the doctors performing the surgery.

The boys were getting big and they loved to go to the park. We loved taking them and making videos. We made them their own YouTube channel. They love airplanes and we had one specific place we went to all the time up at the airport. The boys loved this one park because it was close to the airport and there was a fighter jet that was mounted on a concrete pillar in the middle of the park. We would pack up a lunch and their bikes and head over there. We had a lot of good times there.

This was also the year that I got my German Shepherd. Derek didn't mind spending the $1500 on her at all. I was happy that he was willing to get me a dog. We all welcomed her and the boys loved her. She became our fur baby. Nikki was a gorgeous dog, her parents were champion show dogs. She was our fur baby and we all loved her, especially the boys. Derek taught Nikki her first few tricks and she was a fast learner. This was a huge step for Derek. He never cared much for dogs. Years prior, he had a job in his First Nation community of putting stray dogs down.

North Bay winters are cold and snowy. Unless you have a snowmobile, or enjoy winter activities (which I didn't because it was too cold), there isn't a whole lot to do outside. So Derek found something he could do. He would go outside and make videos of himself shoveling the driveway. He'd add music to it and upload it to social media. A couple years later, our oldest son told us that his friend saw one of Derek's shoveling videos on Canada's Weather Network.

I was still struggling with a lot of insecurities, and never felt good enough for my husband. His wandering eyes always pierced my heart. I didn't look at other men, I honored him. Why couldn't he do the same?

One day I was at the mall eating at the food court. Across the food court sat this beautiful blonde. I mean she was made with special care and was padded in all the right places. She was definitely on a higher level on the scale than I was. I felt ugly and unattractive. Why wasn't I born prettier? I was glad my husband wasn't around to see her because his head would have been on a swivel. But while I watched her the Lord spoke to my heart and said that if I wanted to look like her, and be like her, I could have no part with Him. Her heart was somewhere else. And her eyes were dark and she was pursuing vanity and earthly things. She had an obsession and it was one that could never be fulfilled. I remember thinking about getting breast implants for myself and wondering about ways to improve my body. But the Lord was showing me that vanity was fleeting. And when one has paid and spent fortunes on herself, and in debt, she finds herself still empty. She has traded her life in for something that wasn't real and the companions she finds only desire her for their own pleasure. Those who built their lives on external things are in trouble. They cover their wounds and bruises and yet, they never heal. They are always seeking and looking for validation and find none. But those whose eyes are on Jesus Christ are filled with an abundance of life.

And the life of Christ in me was beyond any earthly beauty. He worked from the inward parts, changing my heart, and His presence in me radiated. As a woman of God, my confidence came from Him. And when you walk with a King, there's a bounce in your step and a glow like no other. It is a beauty that grows and does not fade away because of who He is in me. I was confident in who I was because my identity was in Christ. The more I pursued Him, the more Christ-like I became, and it showed on the outside. I could use makeup or go without it. My beauty came from Him. I no longer was going to look at vanity.

The Lord showed me an image one day that illustrated two different types of women. The first woman built her home on the word of God. She trusted and believed in the word. And inside her home was joy, peace, laughter, love and hope that you could feel and she had a fullness of life in her, and those who lived in her home thrived. And in the other house was a woman who built her home on the lies of the enemy. Her house was full of secrets, jealousy, envy, betrayal, deceit, and murder. It was dark inside and she lived in constant fear of tomorrow. There was no life in that house. It was torment and no rest. And it killed everything in it. But those who build their lives on the rock will endure life's storms (Matt 7:24-27).

Derek

The day following Jesus would go forth into Galilee, and findeth Philip, and saith unto him, Follow me. Now Philip was of Bethsaida, the city of Andrew and Peter. Philip findeth Nathanael, and saith unto him, We have found him, of whom Moses in the law, and the prophets, did write, Jesus of Nazareth, the son of Joseph. And Nathanael said unto him, Can there any good thing come out of Nazareth? Philip saith unto him, Come and see.

Jesus saw Nathanael coming to him, and saith of him, Behold an Israelite indeed, in whom is no guile! Nathanael saith unto him, Whence knowest thou me? Jesus answered and said unto him, Before that Philip called thee, when thou wast under the fig tree, I saw thee. Nathanael answered and saith unto him, Rabbi, thou art the Son of God; thou art the King of Israel. Jesus answered and said unto him, Because I said unto thee, I saw thee under the fig tree, believest thou? Thou shalt see greater things than these. And he saith unto him, Verily, verily, I say unto you, Hereafter ye shall see heaven open, and the angels of God ascending and descending upon the Son of man. (John 1:43-5)

I feel that this passage of scripture accurately describes my journey. It started when I was in Moose Factory early in 2008, just before I met my wife, Sonia. I consider this time when I was "under the fig tree" of religion and works. But even in that time, I had a truly sincere heart and desire to seek and know the Lord.

My intention was to read the entire book of Galatians that afternoon. Not only to read it, but to truly understand it. As I sat there at the kitchen table in my parents' home, I intently read each word over and over until, at last, I was rejoicing as the Word was revealed to me. I was saved by faith! I did not have to earn it. Christ had done it all and I had nothing more to do. That was some time after I had rededicated my life to Christ in 2007. This was the beginning of a journey that led me out of the bondage of religious works and into freedom in Christ.

I was saved by Jesus Christ on August 4, 1990. By faith I had accepted that He was the Savior. And I knew He was my Savior. I had given Him my heart and life. I had been radically and gloriously saved. The power of God had come upon me and I knew He had cleansed me of every sin. I was washed clean and forgiven. I was a new creation. I devoured the Word of God. I worshipped and praised Him. I spent hours in my room reading my Bible, praying, and crying out to Him. I experienced His sweet presence. I was so in love with Him. And because of that hungry heart, He filled me with His presence.

Soon, His presence and anointing would spill out upon others as I worshipped Him in the little church I attended. Church leadership saw the anointing upon my life and I was thrust into a role that I was not ready for. I became a worship leader and soon after I became the church's youth leader. The anointing was present and I began learning how to "lead" a church service. The church leaders took me under their wing and pushed me more toward ministry. I learned through observation how to speak as a church leader. There is a church language that those behind the pulpit use, and I learned how to use it. If the anointing wasn't present, I could use natural emotion, familiar church praise and worship songs, provoke responses with phrases that incited the congregation to praise out of guilt rather than from a heart of love for Him. Without realizing it, I had learned to control the crowd. I had become a religious leader. I had become enslaved.

The snare of religion is that you become good at "acting a part" that looks good to others. You can "act" like a good Christian, pretending that you're living a holy and righteous life. As a church leader, you have to be "above reproach" and that pushes you to appear more righteous than those you are leading. In fact, you can even convince yourself that you're doing very well at being a good Christian. It doesn't take long before you become self-righteous. A perfect Christian who is following Christ – and you believe the deception. It's a perfect snare for the enemy because he can now use your "hypocrisy" to build more snares in your life. Since you are now motivated to appear self-righteous, and you are willing to hide little "slip-ups" or minor characteristic flaws, he will use those for bigger snares. Behind closed doors there is a lie, there is a double life. It wasn't long before I became ensnared and enslaved in sexual immorality.

Times Square Church Pastor, Tim Dilena, shared the following shocking statistics regarding pornography in his Sunday sermon from March 10, 2024. The pornography industry generates more money than the NFL, NBA, and MLB combined. There are over 42 million pornographic websites on the internet, with an estimated 370 million pages of pornography. Of young people aged 18-24, 76% are actively searching porn on their devices daily. Pornography, says Pastor Dilena, is an epidemic in the church today. 68% of all church-going men are actively viewing porn on a regular basis. More shocking is that 50% of all pastors are doing the same. Marriage counselors report that 59% of all counseling sessions are because of husbands who are addicted to pornography.[1]

I found myself shackled in pornography and masturbation. It was not an overnight fall. It was a gradual slope that started with being deceived into believing that I could hide my little sins and act as if I was a "good Christian." The fact was that I was harboring sin in my heart by allowing hypocrisy to take root in my life. I could lead a song service, I could lead the altar call, and as long as no one bothered to sit and talk with me about my prayer life or my alone time, everything was "good." I fell into a cycle of sin, shame and condemnation. I wanted to serve the Lord sincerely, but I was unable to do it with a clear conscience. I was trapped in a snare of self-preservation and religion. Eventually, I was unable to live this lie of a life and I soon turned away from the Lord.

But yet, as I look back, I know that even in that moment, the Lord saw me.

The fig tree is often a description of the religious church. In the Garden of Eden, Adam and Eve tried to hide their "nakedness" from God, and from each other, with fig leaves. The fig tree is the false covering we use to hide our failures and sins from others and from God. Jesus cursed the fig tree when it did not bring forth fruit to satisfy His hunger. It is a picture of the fruit of righteousness and holiness that the Lord wants from His bride. The writer of Hebrews declares to the church that without holiness no man will see the Lord. Jesus Himself said on the Sermon Mount that only the pure in heart would see God. Peter writes that we are to be holy as He is holy. And yet, Paul quotes Isaiah and says that all of our righteousness is as filthy rags. There is nothing good about us, but we try so hard to maintain this veneer of fake righteousness that we become just like the Pharisees who rested on their own laurels of self-righteousness. All of it is just fig leaves in a vain attempt at covering up our sin. To others, we may appear "righteous." Our only hope of righteousness is found in the atoning blood of Jesus Christ. And no amount of self-righteousness can come close to pleasing the Father. In fact, anything other than the blood of His Son Jesus Christ is an abomination to the Lord.

History suggests that while the Hebrew rabbis would teach the Torah to their students, oftentimes they would find shade under a nearby fig tree to teach. Likewise, many students would be found sitting under the fig tree pondering the teachings. These students became enthralled, not with Yahweh, but rather with what the study of Yahweh would give them: power, prestige, and fame. They saw how the masters of the law were treated. They were given the highest honors at the feast tables. They were revered by the crowds. Their outward righteousness was heralded by others. And yet, their evil hearts clamored for the praise and adoration of men. But God was not fooled by this. He saw through the deceit.

The Pharisees of their day had created a complex structure of religious activity that would determine the level of holiness that a person had attained. There were few other sources that a person could learn about the Almighty God. Nathanael had to listen and attend their teachings. And one day, as he sat under the fig tree, Nathanael had a truly "religious" experience with Yahweh. Although he had no other place to turn to learn about God, he wanted to know Him. He had no choice but to sit "under the fig tree" of the Pharisaical teachings to seek Him, but his heart yearned after the Living God. He hungered for truth in the inward parts as the writer of Psalms declared. He wanted to be pure before God. He wanted to be holy. Although he sat under their teachings, his heart truly yearned after knowing God. And I truly wanted to serve the Lord with my whole heart. I wanted to be a true servant of God, but the fig tree of religion I was sitting under had choked me into submission to sin.

For years I struggled. I was what other Christians called a "yo-yo Christian." I was up and down for years. But finally in 2007, I gave up being that up and down Christian and committed my life to the Lord. It was one day at that kitchen table, while studying Galatians, that the Lord saw me "under the fig tree."

A few months later, the Lord sent someone to me. It was the same "Come and see" moment that Nathanael had with Philip. And the one who came for me would not only become my best friend, but would also become my wife.

The first time I saw Sonia was in a picture she had chosen for the promotion of her book *Rise Up My Beloved*. Her smile was incredible!

In it, I saw joy and a glow of the Holy Spirit upon her and it absolutely drew and captivated me. I can only assume that Nathanael saw something similar upon Philip that I saw in Sonia. It was something that totally made me want to seek and know what she had. It was something deep within her. And it was simple: She had found Him – and I hadn't yet. And because of that, I had to "come and see" what she had found. And through our entire marriage, she has continually led me to Him.

Several years after we had been married, after much turmoil and pain, we found ourselves in Yorkton, Saskatchewan. I remember sitting (again at the kitchen table) with my wife discussing childhood memories, when suddenly I was hit with something I had not realized had deeply wounded me.

As a boy, I was a happy and avid learner. I was, for all intents and purposes, a nerd. But at the age of 12, my parents decided to leave the small town of Moose Factory, Ontario, to move the entire family to my mom's home community of Waskaganish, Quebec.

The entire family, that is, except for me.

I was to be left behind to live with my uncle and his family so that I would finish off my grade 8 school year. I really did not have a say in the matter. Some time later, I joined my family in Waskaganish. Up to this time, I had been a straight-A student and was always at or near the top of my class. After this, I no longer wanted to be "a nerd."

I attended my first year of "high school" in Waskaganish, but the curriculum was not challenging enough for me and I lost complete interest in learning. Although they tried to have me moved to a higher grade, my parents and teacher were unable to convince the school administration that I should be moved. And so my parents decided to send me back to Moose Factory the following school year. It was decided that this time I would live with my grandfather. Although I loved the time with my grandfather, it was here that I began a life of drugs and alcohol. I was placed in Advanced level High School courses and I somehow managed to scrape by with good marks although I no longer loved learning.

When the school year ended I was back home with my family in Waskaganish. The following school year, instead of being sent back to my grandfather, I was sent to Val d'Or, Quebec, a tough French mining town in Northern Quebec that had a very blatant racism problem.

My first night in Val d'Or I was placed in a hotel room with an older teen who had spent his summer selling drugs for a local dealer. He was delivering $10,000 to the drug dealer from his summer sales of hashish and cocaine. The drug dealer arrived into our room with cash, hash, and coke. I had never been so high in my whole life. I had never been suspended from school before, but it was during that time that I experienced my first school suspension. The rest of my school year – at least until the day I quit in February – was just a cycle of skipping school, drugs, and drinking.

I was returned to Waskaganish where I continued going deeper and deeper into drugs and partying. Again, the following fall, I was sent away to school. This time I was sent to Hull, Quebec, which sat directly across the river from Ottawa, Ontario. And this would be where I finished my high school years two years later.

I told my wife about the day my classmates received their diplomas. I remember standing by the gymnasium door as they walked across the platform to receive their high school diplomas. Although I had enough credits to graduate and had attended the graduation prom, I was told I would not be participating in the graduation ceremony because of some red tape I knew nothing about. Instead, I walked to a local apartment building and got high, alone. All I remember is the pain of being rejected and alone. No one from my family was there.

It wasn't until that moment many years later, at our kitchen table in Yorkton, Saskatchewan, that the hurt from those years hit me. A flood of pain rose up within me and a deluge of tears filled my eyes. The Lord revealed to me that I had been wounded. All those years of being sent away for education had created an emptiness in me. I had been dealing with a root of rejection for so many years and had not even been slightly aware of it. I now realize that when I had come to the Lord, I had eased and hid the pain with religion. Religion gave me the recognition and acceptance I had yearned for as a child and had been missing as a teenager. Although God had delivered me from drugs and alcohol, I had taken up a new drug, religion. Religion keeps you in bondage. It does nothing to address your wounds. It cannot heal your wounded heart. Only Jesus came to heal the brokenhearted (Luke 4:18). But I had only been using Jesus as a cover for religion. And religion feeds the one thing that God hates above all, pride.

Pride comes in many forms. But it will always promote, preserve, and protect one thing: self. In other words, the flesh. The worship of self is the root of pride. It moves God from the throne of our hearts and places us in His place. If people hurt us, instead of yielding to God's Word, the flesh wants malicious revenge. Thats where I was. My heart was full of anger and malice. I learned that it had come from a wound of rejection that had spawned a root of bitterness in my heart. Here I was faced with the fact that I had been wounded deeply by abandonment. I asked the Lord for forgiveness and for healing. For my healing, I didn't know that I would have to be humbled.

Eight

❧

Like Moses in the Wilderness

We had made the decision to leave Saskatchewan and move to North Bay because my husband had received a phone call from the Chief of his community in Northern Ontario. His community had been involved in a land claims court case with the Cree Nation, the Canadian government, and two provincial governments before we got married. This was something that he had been a part of and when the Chief called from Ontario, my husband felt an obligation to go and help. I had been comfortable with this, but then my husband was nominated for Deputy Chief in his community. We worked on a campaign and my husband was successfully chosen to be the Deputy-Chief. The difficult part was that in order to fulfill the role, we had to move to the community. We had no choice. We had to move. I knew that this move to the north was going to be hard on me at times, but He was going to work in the midst of it. The Lord put this scripture on my heart before leaving:

But the fruit of the Spirit is love, joy, peace, longsuffering, gentle-ness, goodness, faith. (Galatians 5:22)

I often think of the amazing testimony of Corrie Ten Boom. Along with members of her family, she had helped over 800 Dutch Jews escape from the Nazi's. When they were discovered, they were all arrested and put into a concentration camp. Her time in the concentration camp was very difficult. She and her sister were treated very badly by the camp guards. Her sister died in the camp and Corrie Ten Boom was alone. She battled with hatred in her heart against those who had treated them so badly.

Years later, as she travelled the world giving her testimony of how God kept them, she would run into a familiar guard that once tortured her. He had come to hear her speak in one of her meetings. He approached her and asked if she remembered him. And of course, she did. He had come to ask her forgiveness. But she didn't know if she could forgive him, she had to ask the Lord for His help. Once she prayed, she felt His love flow through her for him. I could only imagine a compelling tenderness and meekness in her character, an overflow of the life of Jesus Christ upon her life. What seems impossible to us is possible for Him, if we ask Him.

And this is what He desires for all of us. This was what I was desiring that I could be in a place of absolute trust and dependence on the Lord. I wanted the life of Christ flowing out of my life. He is the River of Living Water and we can drink from Him daily.

I knew moving to an isolated place wasn't going to be easy. I knew it would stretch me and change me. My husband prepared me the best he could. He told me how many people would come to the island and would either come to love it or hate it. Many people, he said, could not handle the isolation. After having been in urban areas where you could jump in a vehicle and drive wherever you needed to it was hard to live in a remote and isolated place. But the land and scenery were beautiful. My husband always said he missed the land. And I understood why when we arrived there.

Moose Factory is a small, isolated island in Northern Ontario. You can only reach Moose Factory by coming to the mainland community of Moosonee. These communities can only be reached by plane or train. There is no road that connects them with the outside world. Once you arrive there, you have to take a boat in the summer, or drive over the frozen river in the wintertime, to the island. Two times a year you can only get there by helicopter as the river freezes or as the river ice begins to melt away. It really is isolated. But it is beautiful.

We moved into a small three-bedroom house and it wasn't long before we settled in that Hasslina wanted to move down south. We have always mainly lived in urban areas so this was a change for all of us. It was a remote island and many of the people still spoke their native Cree language. My husband was fluent in Cree, but I didn't know a word of it. The people still practiced their cultural traditions of harvesting wild game for food. My mother-in-law was traditional in the sense that she had a Cree cooking tent in her backyard. She plucked geese and cooked them over an open fire. That was a whole new experience for me and the kids. Derek loved to eat goose but I wouldn't try it. I've never been one for game meat.

Having goose in the North is like having a roast supper on Sundays. We didn't have it every day but when we did, we enjoyed it. I wondered though if these were the geese my kids and I would feed at the park. I didn't know we were fattening them up before they headed up North to be on someone's kitchen table. I was an urban native and my food came from the grocery stores.

When David had his first birthday, we had a big celebration. It's customary in the Cree culture that when children have their first-year birthday party, they are given a goose leg to chew on. I still have the pictures of David chomping on his first goose leg.

The hardest part of moving up there was being accepted by the community members. Small knit communities keep outsiders out until they can get to know them. I understood that, that was the same for all small places. I knew in time that they would get to know me and I would make a couple of friends. I was more surprised by the response from the church. There were a few that literally looked me up and down as I stood there. I suppose I didn't meet their approval because I was never accepted by some. The word that the Lord gave me came back to me about meekness and gentleness. I knew that this was a time He would use to purify and refine me. I couldn't stay offended by how others treated me. He said that people would know if we were his disciples by our love for one another (John 13:35) so I would love no matter what.

I'd gone through rejection before within my own community but wondered when things would get easier? Would they ever? I was reminded of the woman with the issue of blood (Mark 5:25-34). She had been sick for 12 years and had heard Jesus was coming through town. I didn't have an issue of blood and I wasn't sick, but I wasn't received. Yet I was made to feel like an outcast. I had to contend with these religious voices that called me no good. I had to deal with family and friends who didn't want me around. I had to push through all those religious voices, and those who despised me to keep walking with the Lord Jesus. I knew He received me and that He loved me. I was like that woman. She would not be accepted by many and no one thought of her or wanted to be near her but she knew she had to reach out to Jesus. She heard the news He was coming. And nothing was going to stop her from pursuing Him. And when she touched the hem of his garment she was made whole.

I made the decision a long time ago that nothing was going to stop me from following Him. I knew who I believed in. I had touched Him and He made me whole. I was transformed and washed by the Blood of the Lamb. I have seen, from the rearing of my children to every facet of my life, that I need the River of Life flowing through me. The Word of God is counsel and truth for our lives and I ran to it. There are many, including those who profess to know the Lord, who put their hope in secular teachings and do what other people are doing. Those who press in with the Lord have less in common with those who don't. This reminded me of the time in BC when the Lord told my husband and I that we would be hated for His namesake (Matthew 10:22).

You may not be received by others and you may even feel like an outcast but the Lord won't reject you. Keep going to Him. You may be misunderstood in what you do but you have an honest heart, He sees you.

I had to keep pushing through the religious circles and crowd that would discourage me from going any further. I had to push through the smirks and slander. I was determined and my mind was made up that I was going to pursue Jesus Christ with all that I had.

I loved Moose Factory and the people. We would have liked to have our own boat to go out on the river. Derek shared a story with me about a day when he took his friend and his wife out on the river. He said they saw a storm coming, but they proceeded with their plans anyway. The storm arrived much sooner than they had expected. His friends were in another boat and they wanted to go in one direction, but Derek led them against the wind. And because of his own limited experience on the water with a boat, he possibly averted a tragedy of having their boats swamped and capsized by the storm.

We loved to take walks to the edge of the island and look out on the river. It was beautiful. The sunsets were incredible. I understood why my husband loved the land. Moose Factory had a grocery store, restaurant, plaza and a small strip mall. The community had a Facebook food page and people of the community would sell french fries, poutines and all kinds of food. We ordered a lot of poutines. We decided to make food too. Our oldest son jumped in on it and he made deep fried Snicker bars and panzerottis. We made club sandwiches and fries and those were good. We even offered delivery.

My stepdaughter Kirsten had gone ahead to stay with her grandparents before we moved up north. Even when we moved into our house, she continued to stay with them. She was close to her grandparents and we were not far from them. In fact, we weren't far from anyone on the island. But then came the time when my daughter, Hasslina, wanted to leave and head south to go stay with my mom so she could go to school. We knew we had to let her go because she needed to be closer to medical appointments. She didn't want to be in Moose Factory anymore. This broke my heart and I cried myself to sleep many nights. My heart hurt so badly.

I missed her in the house and it wasn't a quick drive to go see her. Depending on the season it always took planning. Whether that meant catching a water taxi, vehicle taxi, or helicopter to get over the river and off the island, you were limited to your options by the season. Once off the island, you had to catch another taxi on the mainland to get to the airport or train station for all points south. And then finally, if you took the five-hour train ride south and had your vehicle loaded on a train car, you had to unload your vehicle and pack it up for another several-hour road trip. It required a lot of planning, finances and time to go see her.

I could feel His grace being poured deep into my heart during this time. I remember crying to the Lord and pleading my case because it felt so unfair. He could change her heart if he wanted to, He had the power to make her stay. But I sensed deep in my heart that this day was going to come. And I would have to let her go.

His ways were higher than my way, and his thoughts were higher than my thoughts. I had to let her go because there was nothing I could do about it. I cried out, "Lord, it was me that drove my daughter where she wanted to go. I took her to her appointments and to school, it was me that always took care of her!" I was upset that I wasn't the one to be able to do that now. I was here on an island and I wanted to be with her. Both fear and worry tried to overtake my mind about things that could happen to her. I knew my daughter was in good hands and my mother would take care of her, but no one could take care of her like I did. It was then that the Lord answered me, *"It has been me that has kept her, and you, all these years. I gave you that time to be there for her and to be her mother. And I will be there for her now."* Oh how I needed that assurance. It was eye opening for me because in my heart I knew that was true, but I had needed to hear this. He holds each of us in His hands and determines the days we will live. Would I trust the Lord? Would I resent my stepdaughter who was thriving and healthy? Yes, I would trust the Lord because I knew that He loved Hasslina. Things may not have seemed fair, but He knew what He was doing. The Lord was making it uncomfortable for me and it was for my good. It hurt to grow in faith and I didn't like it but I was going to go all the way with Him and draw closer to the Lord.

One day Kirsten had come over. She and Derek had a disagreement over something that her grandparents had allowed her to do and it got very heated. She left angry, upset and in tears. Derek went over to where she was staying with her grandmother to let them know that we were still Kirsten's parents and that they should respect that. It didn't go well. My husband and his mother exchanged words that day.

I remember later watching Derek in the backyard as I was sitting on the deck. He was carving a walking stick and it reminded me of the staff that Moses carried. And it was like the Lord was reminding me of the calling of God upon his life. He would be set apart and for a greater calling than we could imagine. Although he was seething in his anger and at the moment probably hating his life and wanting to die, I saw a man of God coming who the Lord would use. There was an anointing at times when he would minister in word and song. But the enemy would not prosper against him.

After some months, the weight of school and health began to take its toll on my daughter and she needed us to be closer. It was time to head south to be with her. The Lord was leading us out again. This time, Derek knew that he would not return the same man he was before leaving.

My brethren, count it all joy when ye fall into divers temptations; Knowing this, that the trying of your faith worketh patience. But let patience have her perfect work, that ye may be perfect and entire, wanting nothing. (James 1:2-4)

Derek made the announcement that he would be leaving the position of Deputy-Chief and that we would be heading south for the sake of our family. Our move was done quickly. We had sold off our bigger furniture because of the moving expenses. Moving off an isolated island is expensive. We were moving to London, ON.

We found a house in the east end of London with a nice size backyard for the boys. It had a nice big basement for our older ones. When we arrived in London, we didn't have very much furniture. But the Lord provided and when we arrived in London, my friend and her husband jumped in to help us. They asked if they could take our moving truck because they had a few places to go to pick up some furniture. When they came back we had a kitchen table and some end tables. When it was all said and done we had an adorably furnished home.

In the backyard, we found out that there was a family of skunks living under the shed. And how we found out was that our dog Nikki got sprayed by one. My daughter and I went to the movies and I received a text from Derek that Nikki had been sprayed by a skunk. I rushed home to assess the situation and it took my breath away when I got inside. The house stunk bad! Nikki had been sprayed in the face. I quickly drove to the nearest Shoppers Drug Mart for hydrogen peroxide and baking soda. I was going to make a solution to wash Nikki with. As I approached the check out, the lady ahead of me could smell the skunk! It was on my clothes. I paid for my items, and exited the store as quickly as I could.

My husband got a job on the Oneida settlement about 30 km away from London. I used to live there when I was around 12 years old. My mother was married and we moved out there. We were only there for about a year when things went bad in her marriage. I came home from school and the vehicle was packed up and we left. My mom decided that was it. We went to a shelter and we never went back. The life we knew all went downhill from there. It was bittersweet to take a drive out to Oneida with Derek sometimes.

It wasn't long before we started to struggle financially. Derek's salary was nowhere close to what we had in Northern Ontario. I wanted to settle down in London and raise our boys there. The idea of moving again was exhausting and I was done with the packing and going. It felt good to be back where I grew up.

The Lord has put it on my heart to write another book for some time, but I didn't know the core of it. What was the reason for it? I was driving down Cheapside Road in London one day. I asked Him what He wanted me to write about. And I heard one word and that was "discipleship." I got excited about that.

Derek and I had talked about the need for discipleship before. We both had seen how this was lacking in the church. There were many who got saved and they got pushed into ministry. But they didn't know who they were "in the Lord." My husband knew this firsthand. After he had been saved he was put into ministry before being discipled. He had a beautiful anointed voice and leaders used this and put him into ministry before he was ready. And this is happening everywhere. This was an area my husband struggled in because he knew the word of God but could not find freedom. He understood the concept or theology about what it meant to be "saved" but he himself was never discipled. I knew that I had heard from the Lord. I called my husband and my mother to let them both know that I would be writing another book. I knew what the book was going to be about. What I didn't know was what to write, but I knew that the Lord was going to show me.

My two older children seemed to be running farther from the Lord. They were drinking and it hurt my heart to see the direction that they were going because I knew that road wouldn't end well for them if they continued that way. I was up praying and interceding for them through the night when they were out. I had to keep putting them before the Lord.

One night as I was in prayer the Lord spoke to my heart that when He was seeing me in my brokenness He was seeing my children in their pain and He had plans for them too. He wasn't saving me for just "me" but was working in the midst of it all for their sake too. I would minister His Word and encourage my children whenever I had the chance thinking this was the best thing to do for them. But one afternoon while out riding around with Hassan somewhere that all changed. I don't remember our discussion but what he said to me opened my eyes to how I was pushing him away from the gospel and shutting him down from opening up to me.

My son and I have always been close and pushing him away was the last thing I wanted to do. He's a good kid and I so badly wanted to see him on fire for the Lord. His dad, his cousins, aunts and uncles were all Muslims and he contended with enemies I knew nothing about. I couldn't force the timing and moment Hassan would come to serve the Lord. That was all in His timing. My job was loving him and being there for him. My husband told me years before that the Lord spoke to him that Hassan would preach the word. I didn't know when this would happen, but I was hoping it would be soon.

If I could just help the Lord out with that then that would be great. But what Hassan told me that day, shocked me. He told me, "You don't have to always be right," and for the first time in a long time, I had nothing to say. He knew the things I was saying to him were true but he wanted me to listen to him. He didn't want to have to hear me "preach to him."

When did the Lord ever make me the overseer and the one in control of him? He didn't. He called me to pray and intercede. I needed to listen more to what Hassan had to say and what was going on with him in his life. He was an adult now. It was not my job to change him but it was the working of the Holy Spirit. I needed to be a mom and be there for him. Then I could be an effectual praying mom with power and minister His Word against enemies that he was contending with. He was not my enemy. I was trying to make things happen in my husband's heart and in my children but I couldn't do it because I had no power in myself. And it was proving to be very tiring.

We can't part rivers and command the waves and storms to stop. What will we do when we hear the hooves beating down on us and our enemies threatening to crush our heads?

Nine

You Don't Know the Path of the Wind

But if ye bite and devour one another, take heed that ye be not consumed one of another. (Galatians 5:15)

I felt like a prisoner in my own home. We went out but we always knew there was going to be another argument. I was growing bitter and cynical towards my husband. Was it jealousy? Was I a jealous and insecure wife? I didn't want to know what happened in his head or why this spirit of lust was shown to me. I never felt it when he wasn't around. It was better when I was left in ignorance. Ignorance was bliss! It wasn't just a glance at another woman - I could handle that. Temptation came to us all but the spirit of lust came with its vivid images and it used women as objects. I didn't want to be attached to that anymore and my resentment grew. It was hard to listen to anything he said he would do like fasting or praying. He would attempt to pray for the first couple of days or fast but he would soon quit. And nothing came out of what he said.

That moment of "change" finally arrived. We got into a big argument that day and I said the words I had promised I would never say and I kicked him out. I was tired of being hurt. He left on foot and didn't take the vehicle so I assumed that wherever he went, he would come home after a couple of hours but I didn't hear from him. Later that evening, I called him, and he wasn't answering his phone. He didn't have any friends in the area and no family so I expected him home. And like any other argument we had, after things calmed down, you come back together and work it out. We needed to talk and work through this. I was beginning to miss him at home and started to feel concerned for him. It was evening now and it was dark outside. I decided to check our bank account, but there were no withdrawals made. We didn't have much in the account anyway to begin with. What I didn't know was that at the time, he had boarded a bus and was leaving the city. And he had no intention of coming back to me.

I started thinking of places that he could have gone and I contacted his daughter in Ottawa. And she reluctantly told me he was there. They were out at a restaurant eating when I called her. I could tell she was uncomfortable and didn't want to be caught in the middle between me and her dad. I never imagined that this would have happened. I left a message with her for him to call me and he called me a few days later. He called to tell me that it was over and our marriage was done. His voice was cold and I knew he was serious. He said he was looking for a new job and had quit the one he had in Oneida. I was shook to the core and couldn't believe what I was hearing. He had a family! We had two boys to raise! He was married to me! How could he just leave? He was looking for a new place, a new job to start a new life. He hung up on me and from that point on, he stopped talking to me. It was like I was dead to him and I didn't exist anymore.

My boys wanted their daddy home and they cried almost every

night. I was shaken to the core when my youngest son, Joshua, asked me why I told daddy to leave. My heart broke for them and there was nothing that I could do to bring their daddy back. And in their eyes, it was my fault. I knew he didn't understand what had happened, except that mommy made daddy leave. I had to believe and trust in the Lord to bring my husband and their daddy back home.

The evenings were rough and I dreaded the nights. I would be alone and my boys cried every night. After they fell asleep, I felt really alone. The house was quiet. The hardest part of the day was always around the time he would have arrived home from work and we would lay down together in our bed. I would lay in his arms as he held me. He would talk about his day at work and I had much to say about my day with the boys. But now, I dreaded the nights and a new day knowing that I would have to endure it all over again. I felt the complete absence of him gone from the home. I could see him sitting in his favorite spot in the living room and how I wished he were there again. I wondered where he was and if I was on his mind. I was a complete wreck. I didn't know how I was going to get through these coming days. I had no appetite and I couldn't eat. I was losing weight. I made smoothies to keep my health.

One evening, I got a text message from my daughter Hasslina asking me how I was doing. She was out visiting with her dad that evening. I don't remember my response to her but I will never forget her reply. She texted me a Bible verse. I grabbed my Bible, and opened it up.

And all things, whatsoever ye shall ask in prayer, believing, ye shall receive. (Matthew 21:22)

I was shocked to see that because she was the last person I expected to send me a promise from the Lord. My heart was greatly encouraged. It meant everything to me. I needed to hear a word and wanted to feel something other than fear. And from the mouth of babes, His promise came forth. It's that moment when you think your children are not listening that you find out they were. I had to believe with prayer. The Word that came to me was life and I grabbed hold of it and held on to it. I was going to believe for my marriage to be restored. My husband was going to come home.

Maybe you're experiencing this kind of rejection right now and everything seems hopeless. There seems to be no point in going on? How will you endure the days ahead? What will you do?

Every time the phone rang, and it didn't ring often, I always hoped I would hear my husband on the other end. One day I quickly answered my phone when it rang. It was my mother-in-law. My heart shook as she spoke, her voice was cold as she asked me, "Where is my son?" I told her that I didn't know where he was. She asked again and I couldn't tell her because I really didn't know, except that he was in Ottawa. Before she hung up, she said some very unkind things that shocked me. I never expected that from her. Shook up from her call, I called my husband and I asked him what he had told his mother. And I told him what she had said to me. He told me, "I never spoke to her and I definitely would not tell her to say anything like that to you!" And then he hung up on me. I found out later that he had called and very angrily asked her, "What did you say to Sonia? What did you say to her?" And in his anger, he said the same thing to her and told her to stay out of his life. He was so full of anger and rage. When he hung up from that call Derek would not talk to his mother again for a very long time.

The days seemed long and hard. I knew I had to find a place to pray. Wherever I lived I had always sought out a place to pray outside somewhere. I felt closer to the Lord when I prayed. I needed to find a spot. I took a drive to the outskirts of the city, and I found the perfect place. It was down a gravel side road and it was beside a small lake. It was perfect. I felt comforted being there because my husband loved the water. This became my place of solace and it was where I cried and let my tears fall. I yelled out to the Lord and sometimes, screamed. The onslaught of lies that would come to me during the day would occasionally overwhelm me. There were moments where I felt complete dread that this was it for our marriage. I wanted my husband back. I wanted to talk to him and he wouldn't let me in. He wouldn't talk to me no matter what I said to him. When he called it was for the boys and he threatened to hang up on me if I got on the phone. There were days that I cried all the way there. The thought of losing my husband for good scared me. The thought of rearing my boys alone was even scarier. Before I had married Derek, I had been a single parent for years. I knew the hardship and how difficult it was. But my time there in prayer with the Lord gave me strength.

It was time to put my Bible verses up. When I surrendered my life to the Lord at the age of 25, I put Bible verses up everywhere in my living room and in my kitchen. I had handwritten in big cursive writing, "Jesus Saves" in red on my living room wall. I had scriptures that bordered the walls. His Word was powerful and I wanted to know it. I wrote my scriptures on cue cards. I had them in my journal so I could memorize them. There was a new love in my life. And I had no shame in sharing about Him. No one could have told me that Jesus wasn't real. He changed and transformed my life. One of my neighbors told me another neighbor had called me "super spiritual." She said I was "too much with this God thing." Another friend who I used to party with said that he'd heard I had gone "religious." But none of that mattered to me because I knew in whom I believed. I knew what He was doing inside of my heart. I was seeing what He could do in a surrendered life.

He has delivered us from the domain of darkness and transferred us to the kingdom of His beloved Son. (Colossians 1:13)

Before I gave my life to Jesus Christ, my heart was cold and hard. I was given over to alcohol, sex and drugs. I had anxiety, fear and struggled to talk with people. When I talked with anyone, my face would go deep red and I would panic. I couldn't imagine a future. I had no life and merely existed. I was a single parent and didn't know anything about parenting. Until one day, I couldn't do life anymore. I was a single parent with two children. I would look at my children's faces and I knew that I didn't want them to have the same life that I had lived. Was there another way? I knew I had no power to change myself or my circumstances. I knew that there was only one way. I began to seek the Lord. The Spirit of the Lord was with me. He began changing me and healing me. When I put my children to bed upstairs, I would come back down to sit in the living room. I would play some worship music and pray. I would sing and open my heart to Him. The more I sought Him, the more He began to show up.

And ye shall seek me, and find me, when ye shall search for me with all your heart. (Jeremiah 29:13)

My tears flowed freely and times of refreshing came. His Word was truth and I wanted more. The Bible verses began to go up on my walls. They went up in my living room and kitchen. There was power and life in His Word. With each new passage of scripture I began meditating on, it chiseled off more and more of the hardness in my heart. I began to feel hope and love that I had never known before in my heart. I had always felt ashamed of being Indigenous. I felt shame because of the things that I had done in my past. Now this life inside of me, His presence living in me, was setting me free!! Jesus was real! I wanted to run to every house that I could and tell them that He was real! He is perfect in all His ways. He was both 100% man and God. The Word of God had become flesh and

He walked among us. His Word to me was like holding a mirror up in front of me and seeing who I was on the inside. It called me to repent and to turn from my sin. His righteousness and holiness was what I wanted and desired. I wanted more of Him.

And now, in this time we were facing, I went running to His promises again because everything I had depended on it. I had anger and hurt in my heart and I was holding on to it. I didn't want to continue to go on in the ways things were. I needed His counsel and His truth. We needed His power and life in us and in our home. I searched His Word and began putting them down on construction paper. I taped them on our bedroom wall and wrote out in big letters again that said, "Restore My Marriage Jesus". I knew if anyone could bring my husband home, it was going to be Him. I continued doing this day after day, week after week. I posted up Bible promise after Bible promise for my husband and my marriage. I posted up our marriage verse among them.

And that he died for all, that they which live should not hence-forth live unto themselves, but unto him which died for them, and rose again. (2 Corinthians 5:15)

My husband knew this truth and to abandon me would mean to abandon the Lord. We chose this verse because this was what we decided to do and this was to live for Him and not live for ourselves. It is a dangerous thing to live and move in your own understanding. We had to move towards the truth and obey Him. I had to pray and trust the Lord for my husband.

and the Spirit of the LORD will come upon thee, and thou shalt prophesy with them, and shalt be turned into another man. (1 Samuel 1:6)

I was waiting for that man of God to come forth, the one I knew the Lord had preserved and kept for this time. But he was running and in rebellion. I told the Lord, "He loved you and he's blind right now. Lord, only you can grab hold of His heart."

I prayed John 17 over my husband and our home. It was a conversation between Jesus and the Father. I saw that the Father had given men to the Lord on earth and He would keep them as the Father and Him were one. We would also be one with them. I would pray this chapter and hold on to this promise. "Lord you have the power to keep my husband. Only You can save him. Show Him your love and your goodness. Remind him from where You pulled him out from."

I went out to my spot everyday. I knew the Lord was moving. But I remember one of my lowest days where every lie came against my mind. It was the lie that I was going to be alone again. My husband still wasn't talking to me. And the longer the days carried on, it felt like there was no hope. At times, it seemed easier to just quit and give up.

One night after taking my oldest son to work I pulled into my driveway and I was feeling the pressure of everything. How was I going to survive? I would have to move out of this house because I couldn't support all of us with no income. I didn't have next month's rent and I didn't know what I was going to do. My mind was being battered that everything was over between us and the thought of being alone hit me again. I thought that it would be better to hand the boys over to their dad to raise because they would have what they needed. I called my mom and she encouraged me to keep going. She encouraged me not to give up.

It was then I saw the crossroad that my mother had come to herself many years ago. If I surrendered my boys, history would repeat itself. My boys would feel hurt and rejected by me. When my mother's marriage broke down she gave up my little brothers to their dad thinking it was the best thing for them. But it was probably the worst thing that she could have done. Soon after she did this, she hit the booze hard. Our home fell apart. My mother basically gave up because of the heartbreak of losing her sons. If I did the same, I would fall away too under the crushing weight of losing my boys. I knew I couldn't be without them. I dropped to my knees in surrender years before for my older children and they were the reason I gave my life to the Lord. My boys would be the reason I would drop to my knees again.

History always repeats itself. What happened to our parents will one day visit us down the road. We can cut off generational curses by walking in obedience to the Lord. I had a choice to make.

A few days later, I remember walking into our bedroom and feeling like I was going to have a total breakdown. I felt the crushing weight of being alone again and told the Lord, "I need to hear from you, I don't want to hear another sermon." I didn't want to talk to anyone. "I need to hear from you Lord! Please speak to my heart," I cried. I was so broken. I missed and longed for my husband. I felt the weight crashing down on me again. I went and picked up my Bible. I sat down on the edge of my bed and opened my Bible believing that He would speak to me. I started going through the pages and I came across a Word that spoke directly to me. I knew He was answering me and that the Lord was giving me a promise. The tears began rolling down my cheeks. I missed my husband so much.

As you do not know the path of the wind, or how the bones are formed in a mother's womb, so you cannot understand the work of God, the Maker of all things. (Ecclesiastes 11:6)

I felt Him speaking to my heart, "You don't know how I do things but I am working it out." I felt assurance in my heart that in time, my husband would be home again. My marriage would be restored.

I didn't know how He was going to do it, but I had His Word to hold on to. It was a beautiful passage of scripture. We can't see the answers to our prayers at times. Yet, just like life that is formed in the womb, it's miraculous and unseen, but the answer will come.

There were times I felt as if I were on a spiritual roller coaster with many ups and downs. It was hard to endure each day but I kept busy with the kids. I had my oldest son who was still living at home with me. I would run him to work each day and this kept me busy. My daughter who was home with me also watched the boys when I would go to my place to pray when she wasn't with her dad. Then I had a breakthrough and a moment with the Lord that changed everything.

I drove out to my usual spot, and when I got there, I got out of the vehicle and started walking down the gravel road. Most days I couldn't wait to get out there so I could let it all go. I started crying and releasing everything from that day. I felt a fear and pain unlike anything I'd ever experienced. It felt as if my life was being drained from me. All I wanted was my husband home. How much longer would this last? The lie that would come was that my husband would find a good job and get a new place of his own. I couldn't give room to those thoughts because they scared me so bad. Derek still wasn't talking to me. How could he completely shut me out? As I walked and prayed, with tears streaming from my eyes, The Lord gave me a vision. I looked ahead and saw an immense and incredible darkness in the distance. Though it looked menacing, it could not come any closer to me. I knew that the Lord was holding it all back by the power of His Word and by prayer. Just like the dirt road I was walking on, I may have been only one tiny speck of dust, but His Word was both my shelter and my weapon. His Word kept at bay the plans of the enemy. His Word had power and authority over every plan and evil thing that the enemy wanted to do to me. That day, I saw how incredible His Word was. I knew that as long as I continued to pray and cling to Him I had victory. I would keep praying and trusting in Him. He is God, He is Elohim, all-powerful, omnipotent, omniscient and omnipresent. He was with my husband and He was working in his heart. He was going to restore and renew all things.

Don't quit! Don't give up!! There are too many who quit and throw in the towel before that breakthrough comes. The enemy is the father of all lies and there is no truth in him (John 8:44). He will spew every lie from hell to make you doubt the promises of God. He will have you question the Lord and His promises. The devil is a liar and a deceiver. And he has drawn many away from what the Lord wanted for them. It started in the Garden of Eden when the enemy came to Eve and tempted her. Did God "really" say that? He made her doubt His goodness and His love for her. And put it in her mind that she could do as she wanted and that she would be wise. He blinded her vision and she went in and ate from where she was forbidden to eat from. It's the same lie that many are believing today. "This is my life and I can do what I want." "If the Lord loved me then why am I in this place?" "His promises are for others, not for me!" And because they believe these lies, they walk in rebellion against God and do their own thing.

I loved my husband. I loved my family. If I gave up on my marriage, and stopped believing the Lord's Word for my life, this would have opened the doors for the enemy to come in and destroy my home. He could have my children and all that the Lord had planned for our lives. I didn't know what lay ahead but I wasn't going to give up. Like Nehemiah who stayed the course and didn't allow the enemies to come sway him to move from his position, I was going to stand firm on the promises of God.

Who was Nehemiah?
Nehemiah was a cupbearer for the king of Persia. His brethren and other men who were from Judah came to Shushan palace. When Nehemiah saw them he asked them about those who had been left

in captivity. Nehemiah's heart cried out when they told him that the walls of Jerusalem were broken down and burned. They told him that the people were in great affliction and reproach. When he heard of all this he wept, fasted and prayed before God. His heart was broken (Nehemiah 1:2-3). He repented for the sins of the people and cried out day and night for them and prayed that the Lord would answer him. He took wine to the king who saw Nehemiah's sad countenance and asked him about it. Nehemiah was risking his life by approaching the king with a sad countenance. No one was to enter the king's court with sadness. But the Lord gave favor to Nehemiah when he told the King that his father's city was destroyed and that the walls were burned down. The king granted Nehemiah's request to go back to Jerusalem and re-build the wall.

There are three things we can glean from Nehemiah. The first, was his heart. Nehemiah was burdened to pray for Israel. His heart was troubled and he was in distress about the condition of the city of Jerusalem. He fasted and cried out for them.

Secondly, he had courage. He went knowing that he would have opposition. He knew he would look foolish to some. I am sure there were voices telling him he couldn't do it. Who was he? And what could he possibly do as a cupbearer? He didn't have an army nor was he a king. He was no one significant, but he knew he had to go.

The third thing was his perseverance. He did not give heed to the opposition. He didn't fear those who came against him and mocked what he did. His enemies did whatever they could to try and stop him from rebuilding the wall. They made fun of him and became angry with him. Who did he think he was? What Nehemiah planned to do was too big for him. They told him that if foxes climbed his wall they could bring it down. In Nehemiah, we see a leader who had a purpose and a plan. He knew the enemy would come, but he never lost his focus. The wall was restored in 52 days.

What I love about Nehemiah was that he stood on watch and he had others build alongside him. Likewise, we also need to build our prayer walls. We are building for one purpose and that is to keep out the enemy and his attacks from our homes and our lives. Day and night we are to stand watch and continuously build our walls.

> *Nevertheless we made our prayer to our God, and because of them we set a watch against them day and night. (Nehemiah 4:9)*

Ten

An Ambassador in Chains

It was getting close to Christmas and I was hoping that my husband would come to see our sons. He began to talk to me again to let me know that he was going to come and see the boys. He applied for training to drive haul trucks and would leave for BC, after his visit. He told me that when he came he would be getting a room close by. I was crushed again that he didn't want to stay with me. He almost didn't come, but he did, and true to his word, he stayed in a room close to our house. I remember the day he came and how hard it was for me to keep my distance from him. I wanted to run toward him and throw my arms around him. But I knew he didn't want to be around me. He picked up the boys, and he took them out. But not long after they left, he called to say that his back almost gave out while he was walking out of the store. He wanted to know if I could go with them to McDonald's that way I would be there, if it gave out. Derek has always had a bad back. And when it gave out it usually meant a trip to the emergency room for medication. I jumped on the invitation to go with them to McDonald's and saw this as my chance to possibly talk to him. He came and we went to McDonald's.

While we were sitting at the restaurant, the boys were playing on the playground, the word "baby" slipped from Derek's mouth when he was talking to me. I looked at him and he looked at me but carried on as if nothing happened, but we knew what happened. At that point I knew he still loved me and he was fighting hard against me. How could he fight when he had his wife and sons playing in front of him? We had been blessed with a beautiful family.

We stopped for Chinese food at one of our favorite Chinese places. We went in and we sat down at one of the tables to wait for our food. Derek sat across from me facing the door. And the moment a woman came through the door, his eyes went up and down her like he was going to devour her. He had no regard for me and I couldn't believe how much he disrespected me. He was so bound to lust. It consumed him. We had our food and we left. I didn't say anything to him about what he did or how he made me feel. To him we were done and our marriage was finished.

Christmas morning arrived, and he brought gifts for the boys, and he brought one for me. I was surprised to see one for me since he was making it clear that he wanted nothing to do with me. I asked him to stay for supper and much to my surprise, he accepted. This had to be a good sign that he was coming for supper. I planned to dress my best and give him something to think about. I needed him to see what he had in front of him and remember the good times we had. I wore a nice white shirt and really took time that day to look extra pretty for him. He always called me beautiful and in his own words, I was his "hot iron". I wondered if he remembered. One summer, a few years before, we were at a camp meeting when my husband and I were called up to share a word. While he was up there talking he referred to me as being his iron, and how we sharpen one another, but it slipped and he called me his "hot iron" and that gave everyone a big laugh.

I asked him if we could go for a drive. That was something we always did and while we were out, I noticed he didn't have his wedding band on anymore. That hurt to the core. I asked him if he still had his ring and he said yes, it was in his bag. I still had my rings on and had no intention of taking them off because I was trusting the Lord for my marriage and that he would be home soon. But while we were driving around, Derek told me something that had happened to him one day when he was on the city bus in Ottawa. He said what came back to him was the time in Saskatchewan when the Lord spoke to us as we were out on one of our drives. He remembered how the Lord had told us that Satan desired to sift us as wheat. Derek wasn't sure if it was him or the Lord but he brushed it off and didn't think about it anymore. I didn't know what to say because I was so encouraged by how the Lord was moving in the midst. But I knew the Lord was speaking to him. He may have doubted it but it was not enough for him to not tell me about it. That word did not leave him alone.

Then came the Christmas dinner and it was time to eat. I made a big dinner with all the trimmings. And if I didn't grab his attention, the food for his belly was going to. We all sat at the kitchen table, and like always, we said grace. I could see in his posture and on his face that he was beginning to break down, his face seemed softer and his voice became tender again. The boys talked and were excited about their daddy being home and for a few minutes things felt like they were normal again and we were happy. After supper, I took him to our bedroom and showed him what I had done with the scriptures. He looked at it and he walked away. I could tell he wasn't happy about it. I later found out that he got angry when he saw the wall and he wanted to tear it down.

Later that evening when he was going to head back to his room, his back started to act up and was causing him a lot of pain. He could barely stand or walk. I asked him to stay the night with me and he reluctantly said 'ok.' It was awkward and not much was said that night. We went to sleep and I knew he was still fighting a losing battle. Derek was home. But it was going to take some time before things began to feel okay again. He was still distant and cold.

A day or two later as we were laying in bed he looked up at the wall above our bed. He said to me, "You built a wall here." He was referring to when Nehemiah had rebuilt the wall in Jerusalem. He said, "You never gave up praying." I hadn't seen what he was seeing until then. It all made sense!

Before Derek had left, the Lord kept showing me Nehemiah. It came through sermons or devotions. I even had a close sister in the Lord who named her son Nehemiah! On top of it all, the last time I ministered, before he left, it was about Nehemiah. I had no idea that the word that I had ministered to others would come to test my home. But there it was, I had built up a wall. Just like Nehemiah. I had been praying over our home and our marriage. When opposition came and the voices said my prayers weren't doing anything, that I would be a single parent again, or that it was too late for my marriage and that my husband was going to cheat on me, I believed God's Word and continued to pray.

He left to B.C. for his Haul Truck training. I knew this was going to be difficult but at least I knew he was coming home after that. It was a hard few weeks but he made it back. He found a job on the outskirts of London, not far and started driving a rock truck for a heavy equipment company in a nearby city. It was something he wanted to do. A rock truck was a massive piece of machinery that is used in mining. It would be this time alone in the cab of the truck that the Lord would begin speaking to his heart. He was able to listen to sermons and music while he drove the truck. It was just him and the Lord.

As I reflect back to this time, the mining represented how the Lord went seeking after Derek. He was a diamond in the rough. A treasure like a diamond is found in the ground but when it is found, it isn't found sparkling and shining, it has to go through a process. The diamond is first crushed and then scrubbed until you uncover what lies beneath. Derek saw himself as worthless, but I saw more than what he saw in himself. I knew he was worth the wait because the Lord was bringing forth a diamond.

One day while he was at work a sermon by Carter Conlon entitled, *Ambassadors in Chains* began to play. The service was on a Tuesday night prayer service. The pastor would always share a few of the hundreds – if not thousands – of prayer requests that came in by text. As Derek listened he heard a prayer request that he knew was mine. The odds of the pastor sharing my prayer request was only God! Derek knew it was mine because of the specific details of the request. I had sent in a prayer request saying that my husband left me and my sons. He had been gone 16 days and he wouldn't talk to me and our sons were having a hard time coping. But the most amazing part of this sermon was that it was delivered on Derek's birthday! When he heard the message he knew undoubtedly that the Lord was moving on our behalf. This really spoke to him. There are no coincidences with the Lord. We knew that He was making himself visible to us to show us that His hand was with us and upon us. He was going to do a new thing.

But it wasn't long before we fell back into routine again. I had my husband home and I had to trust the Lord and not be moved by the things I saw anymore in the battle he was in because I had a battle of my own. I was learning all the more that my husband could not be my everything. He could not fulfill me like the Lord could. That was too much to put on any man and the Lord just wanted me to pray and love Derek in spite of his failings and shortcomings as a husband. I knew the Lord was doing a deep work within my own heart in all of this too. We didn't walk by faith, but by sight. This was proving to be a long and difficult lesson to learn.

During the time Derek was gone, I bought a book entitled *Marriage On The Rock* by Jimmy Evans.[2] I highly recommend this book if you're struggling in your marriage. It really shed light on one area I needed to see: *my husband cannot fulfill my deepest need, only the Lord can.* Expecting your spouse to fulfill your innermost needs is to expect too much from them. The Lord is the only one who can fulfill the deepest desires and needs of your life. He knows you better than anyone else does. Let Him disciple you so that you may be firmly planted in your identity in Him.

PART THREE

Go, Love As I Love

Then said the LORD unto me, Go yet, love a woman beloved of her
friend, yet an adulteress, according to the love of the LORD...
Hosea 3:1

Eleven

100 Days Walking By Faith

We began to have sewage and plumbing problems in the house and they were not small problems. We were concerned the basement would flood and the landlord wasn't doing anything to fix the problem. We had no choice but to find another place.

We gave our 60 days' notice and began looking for a new place. Our search did not go well. We had a difficult time finding a place within our budget. We were either passed over as tenants, or the rent was too high. Postponing our move wasn't possible. New tenants had already been found for our house and we had to move. We had to pack and that was a rough process. With two little boys and only a handful of hours in a day it was a stressful move.

On the day of our move, the new tenants were waiting outside for us to move out. We had been taking the last few things left in the house into the vehicle and U-Haul. We knew we had to be out by lunch and we were still trying to move and clean. I always tried to have the house clean before we moved out. The people that were waiting finally came in and asked if I needed help. The wife grabbed a broom and started helping. I was definitely feeling the pressure. But we were finally out of that house and the car was packed up with no spaces to fill. With Derek driving, me in the passenger seat, and the kids crunched up with the pets in the back, we were off. We were so happy to be done with the move and wanted to rest. We laughed and chatted about the last little things we all had to do and did. Then after a driving a few blocks the vehicle suddenly got very quiet. I mean you could have heard a pin drop because the thought probably occurred to us all at the same time, 'Now what?' We didn't know where we were going. Nobody said anything for a few minutes. We had no plan and no idea of what we were going to do next.

We headed over to the discount motels on the east end of London. This would be our home for about two weeks. My brother who lived in London had just been approved for a subsidized home, but he was not yet ready to move in. He offered us to stay at his place until he could get moved in. This was only God because we couldn't afford another week at the motel. We stayed at his house for a couple of weeks. The place had no appliances and a friend of ours purchased a mini-fridge and gave us some money. We were so thankful for His provision for us.

After about four weeks without a place of our own, we found a small townhouse across town on Southdale Road. It was just up the street from where I used to live when I was around 15 years old. This brought back memories of when my mother's marriage fell apart.

After she left her marriage, my mom moved us all there from Oneida. It was from this point that our lives began to fall apart and things would never be the same. My mom cleaned houses to provide for us and she always made sure to have fresh fruit on the table everyday. She did her best to keep us together but it all caught up with her and the stress of rearing the four of us was too much. We had this big brown boat for a vehicle and, although it was a clunker, it took us where we had to go. The boys no longer had a male figure in the house and so it wasn't too long that the police started showing up at our home looking for my brothers. They were becoming too much for my mom to handle. She felt it was better to give them up to their dad as he could provide for them better than she could. It was the last place that felt like a home before things turned from good to very bad. My mother was unable to deal with the pain of losing her boys. She began drinking again and our home was no longer the same.

As my husband and I settled our family into the little town-house on Southdale, I started to have health issues. I wasn't feeling well anymore. I felt lethargic. I had headaches. And I felt tired all the time. My hips were hurting again. I had pain sleeping on my side and I would flip like a fish throughout the night. I went to the doctor and he ordered some blood work. When I went back to the doctor's office the nurse told me that I was prediabetic and had high blood pressure. She turned to me and said, "You can still turn this around," and she was right. Did I want to stay in this place? I knew I didn't want to be sick and become a diabetic. I had my boys to think about and I had to stay healthy for them. The choice was mine. I could do something about it or continue on what I was doing. But I knew I couldn't do this on my own. I had tried many times to lose weight. I couldn't do it. I ran to the Lord to help me. "Lord, I can't do this without you. What do I need to do?" And the answer came. And it was very clear.

The Lord instructed me to walk 100 consecutive days! And to stay accountable I would need to share about it everyday online. I knew the Lord had shown me what I had to do.

My husband mapped out a walking route for me and I started walking every evening. I downloaded a Bible and music app on my phone. I would listen to a sermon, or a reading of a Bible chapter, and end the walk by listening to worship music. The Lord fed me each day and I would come home encouraged and would share with others. I knew this time was different because I felt the Lord with me. When it came to exercise or diet before, I had a hard time sticking to it. But now I was coming into the house differently. When I came home, I would do a live video and share what the Lord spoke to my heart. On day three, as I lay in bed that night, the realization of what I had committed to do hit me. I still had 97 days more to go. I yelled out to my husband, "What did I do? What was I thinking when I started doing this walk?" The incredulity in my voice made us both laugh. But what could I do? I had committed to it. There was no turning back. I had a long way to go but I was going to do it. It was done and so we went back to bed.

It was amazing to see where He had moved us and how I was back in the very same area where I grew up. It was bittersweet to pass by that familiar townhouse every day of my walk. It was the last home I had where my siblings and I were all together. One night, as I passed by, a memory came flooding back of how I used to dance carefree upstairs in my room. Oh how I loved to dance! That is, until it occurred to me that I was visible to those outside. I quickly stopped dancing because I only had a sheer curtain and I was embarrassed that I probably had been seen. But those memories were precious and it would make me smile each time I passed by the same window. I remembered that little girl who swirled and kicked her legs in the air with no care in the world. My brothers would be out riding their bikes in the back or creating a ruckus inside the house. Those were beautiful memories before everything had come crashing down around us.

One night, while I was out walking, the Lord began to show me other women were going to come and walk along with me in the *100 Days Walking By Faith* journey. I could see sisters, mothers and grandmothers coming and laying hold of the promises of God for their families. There were going to be many who would get up and move to do what the Lord called them to do. The journey he was putting me on was for the sake of others. In the dead cold of winter, I walked. When it rained, I walked. No matter what I had to face, I was committed to this walk and I was going to face it daily. I was learning to become more disciplined and He was teaching me to persevere.

One evening, during an icy walk, I almost slipped and I told my husband about this. He purchased ice cleats for the bottom of my shoes so that I wouldn't slip again. I recall the first time I wore them. It was right after a fresh blanket of snow had fallen. I walked halfway around the block before I noticed something. Under that fresh snow was solid ice. I would have undoubtedly fallen if not for the cleats I had on. My cleats kept me from slipping and injuring myself. In this, I saw how the Lord keeps us from falling when we can't see the danger. He protects us from things we can't see. My walk everyday, while listening to His Word either by the Bible app or a sermon, was giving me hope and stirring my heart. My prayer life was becoming passionate again and I was abounding in my faith. His Word in me was compelling me to move! What was He going to speak to my heart about today? What was He going to show me? I was abounding in my faith and there were times that I wanted to dance because of the joy of the Lord inside of me. As long as I kept moving and putting one foot in front of the other, He would give me the grace and the power to walk. And every time I got home and made it through those front doors, I felt good!

I remember one day as I was out walking the Lord spoke to my heart that *man will not live by bread alone but by every word that proceeds out of the mouth of God* (Matthew 4:4). We were not going to make it without Him, or without knowing His Word. His Word is a lamp unto our feet and light for our path. It is counsel and instruction on how to live our lives. His Word restores and brings refreshing. He wants us to be established and grounded so that we may walk and move in Him and have our being in Him. Like the prophet Jeremiah, *there is a fire shut up in my bones and I cannot contain it! (Jeremiah 20:9)* What goes in will come out. I wanted more of His Word. There is a song I once heard that has the line, "You haven't lived until you walk by faith." And this was truly happening to me. His Word was going deep and it was transforming me! When we receive His Word in, He moves things out the door like unbelief, fear, passivity – all the things that were weighing me down.

After completing my first *100 Days Walking By Faith*, I lost 20 pounds and 18 inches. I was no longer pre-diabetic and my blood pressure was good. And it felt good. Beyond just the physical bene-fits, I felt something so deep in my heart. A substance of faith that I could feel. I was learning endurance and perseverance through my struggles. I was passionate and falling in love more with my Savior. I was feeling hope again for our marriage and love for my husband. I wanted nothing more than to know His Word and His promises. I had to keep going. I wanted all that He had for me. There were no shortcuts.

One night as I was on my walk I was coming up to the inter-section where I would cross the road. I was about half a block away from the intersection where I would usually cross. I saw that there were no cars in either direction and I thought about darting across the street rather than going to the corner and waiting for the light. But I felt the Lord speak to me, "Keep going to the corner. There are no shortcuts." How would I be able to say I walked 2 miles that evening if I took a shortcut? And so, I kept going to the corner. It was in these moments of obedience, that the Lord was instructing me how to live my life before Him. Especially in secret. Nobody would have known that I didn't walk to the corner and, to some, it might not seem like a big deal. But it is important to the Lord how we live our lives when no one is watching. And He will bless our obedience. He was deepening my character and integrity. There were people who were watching my life. I had a friend and sister in the Lord who watched my posts everyday. It encouraged her and others to see me pursuing Jesus Christ. And He was faithful to give me a word to share each day with people. With each day that I did it, I found that getting online and sharing the gospel was becoming easier. The Lord was giving me courage and confidence. I used to struggle with anxiety and if someone had told me back then that I would be sharing by ministering online one day, I wouldn't have believed it.

I cried out for my prodigal children daily. I was pouring the gospel into my daughter every chance I could get. I knew something was happening in her that was not visible to the eyes. We can't see the roots of the tree but we know they are there and they run deep. The bigger the tree, the deeper the roots may grow. Our oldest son was still doing a lot of drinking. There were many nights that I stayed up pacing the floor praying. I was continually crying out to the Lord.

> *Remember the word to Your servant, Upon which You have caused me to hope. (Psalm 119:49)*

My boys kept me busy. But we knew the Lord was closing doors for us in London. It was becoming discouraging. It was time to look for another job because my husband's salary was not enough. It was important for me to be home with our boys but we needed two incomes to survive. I tried several places to get a job. We didn't like the thought of having anyone else watch our sons. The roles that we both had in our marriage worked for us. My husband was the head of the house. And not in a controlling or possessive way. It is the divine order of the family that the Lord has made for the husband to take and it was his role. He is the head of the house and the Lord would be the head of him. I had to submit to my husband. Now hear me out, I would have had a problem with this before understanding this powerful revelation but there is incredible power when we get out of God's way and let Him do what He wants to do. I needed my husband to take that role because I knew I could not.

One day in my frustration, I told my husband that I was not going to be his mother, but I was his wife. I would not tell him what to do! There were times that he would take a passive aggressive role and this passivity hurt our home. By submitting to him, this allowed him to feel, and to act, like the man of his home. I watched the way I spoke to him. He was my husband and I respected him and honored him. And when the order of God is in place, He can freely move! I knew that if I tried to control my husband and things at home that I would hinder what the Lord wanted to do in him and in me. I embraced the traditional role of a housewife. I know quite a lot of women may want to cringe at this position of being a stay-at-home mom, but I was beginning to see how valuable I was at home. I was a mom and wife who spent my time in prayer and fasting for my family. It was an honor to rear up these gifts that the Lord placed in my hand. One day I would have to answer to Him for what I did with them. The family is God's most treasured institution and I saw why Satan is out to destroy the family, because everything comes from the sanctity of the home. If we have trauma as children we tend to repeat it. If love and joy is in the home, then it too shall be repeated. We will reap what we sow.

Behold the fowls of the air: for they sow not, neither do they reap, nor gather into barns; yet your heavenly Father feedeth them. Are ye not much better than they? (Matthew 6:26)

Though we were facing a difficult financial season, the Lord used our neighbor to remind us that He will keep us. Every morning, she would put out bird seed, nuts and fruits. From the front door of our townhouse, I could see the mixture of seeds, nuts and fruits that lined the sidewalk. The birds always ate good. All the neighboring animals, including skunks, came for the food. I would watch in amazement as the birds swooped down to get their food. I found the birds so delicate, graceful and beautiful. We were struggling and visiting food banks but, through my neighbor, the Lord would speak to me that He was watching over us. He was reassuring me that everything would be okay, even when our vehicle was repossessed. Yes, that was a rough day. But we still had much to be thankful for.

Saskatchewan 2019

As much as we wanted to stay it was pretty evident that we could no longer stay in London. We had no vehicle and Derek could no longer make his way out to work. We couldn't afford to live where we were anymore. We had to leave. And we once again decided to head to Yorkton. We packed what we could in a minivan and trailer and we hit the road west to Saskatchewan. We moved into a unit directly beside my mother's. We didn't have a vehicle anymore so finding a place beside her was only the Lord's doing. Whenever we needed to make a run for groceries or errands, my mom would always let us use her vehicle. She has always been a blessing to us and the Lord put her there again to help us in a time we needed help.

Before leaving Ontario I had applied to the local college in Yorkton to attend a Bachelor of Social Work program. We found a church and we both found jobs working in the same organization. My husband was hired as a Family Finder Recruiter for a native Child & Family Services organization. A few months later, I was hired as an Emergency On-Call Worker. Derek's position required him to find families for native children who had been apprehended by the province. His goal was to find families that were related to the child that would allow the child to continue living near to family and their communities. My job was to apprehend children who might have been in situations of abuse or neglect. Each time I was on-call Derek and I would pray for peace in the communities that I was on-call for. And each and every time, I would always have a quiet week of being on-call.

We soon fell into a regular routine. I homeschooled my boys and went to classes. I was happy to be back in the province because it was home. At the same time, I wasn't too happy because this was where I had experienced the most hurt. It was bittersweet. I had been hurt by my family and by the church.

I knew that I had to walk in love despite what they had done to me and how they had treated me. I was going to choose to walk in love no matter what. This reminded me of the word the Lord spoke to us in the first year of our marriage. We would be hated by all men, for His name's sake. We knew that whatever the Lord called us to do, we were going to be hated. I was going through this now with my family and it wasn't easy.

My husband and I are the same in so many ways, but yet so different. He was brought up in the church his whole life and it made him hard and religious. The Lord brought him out of it to separate him unto Himself and to teach him. I was brought up in a dysfunctional home without church but sought out church and got wounded by it. And I believe that the Lord allowed this to happen so that our lives could be used for His glory to speak to those in similar places as we were in.

I hadn't been back to the province since my book, *Rise Up My Beloved*, was published. I was hoping and praying for reconciliation with my family but that never came. That was apparent one Saturday afternoon. For the sake of protecting my loved ones I won't get into much details of that day.

I was invited out on a Saturday morning to go to a community garden. The day was beautiful. The weather was perfect and the sun was shining. I couldn't have asked for a more beautiful day. When

I got out of my vehicle to meet my family, a little cousin of mine, who was around eight years old, yelled out, "Ewwwww! She's here!?" I knew everyone heard what was said to me and I couldn't move. I had no words. I wanted to disappear and leave. I didn't blame him. Kids only say and repeat what they hear. It just revealed to me that they were still talking about me, and it wasn't good things they were saying. I ran to the Lord in that moment to hold me so that I wouldn't fall apart right there. I could feel my chest swelling up from the shame and embarrassment. My only crime was standing for truth of the gospel. I didn't believe in the prosperity gospel message that my family believed in. I have no regrets because I have decided in my heart I will stand in the old gospel tradition of taking up our crosses and dying to the flesh. I knew I had to press in and keep going. And I wouldn't allow offense to take root in my heart either. Jesus said that offense will come but to endure. I wasn't responsible for what they did, but I was accountable for the things I did. I was going to love them no matter what. And I pray for them continuously and believe that one day we shall all rejoice together in heaven.

Twelve

Behold, I Will Do A New Thing

Behold, I will do a new thing; now it shall spring forth; shall ye not know it? I will even make a way in the wilderness, and rivers in the desert. (Isaiah 43:19)

This verse was written on a whiteboard in our living room. It stayed on that whiteboard for a long time and I was holding on to that promise. Yes, things were hard and we couldn't see what was happening, but He was able to feed us and keep us in these times.

There were some hard times ahead, but something else we never saw coming was just around the corner.

My daughter's behavior had started to spiral downward. She had been going down a dark road of drugs and alcohol at this point in her life. She was beginning to do things that were totally out of character and risky. I began to reflect on the things I did when I was her age, and the thought of it all made me freak out! Would I experience days like when my mom didn't know where I was? Would

I be faced with not knowing where my daughter was? I had to hold on to the Word and His promises. She would not do the things I did. I had to keep believing and holding on to His Word and His promises for her and my family. There were nights when I would check to see if she was home or not. And when I found her room empty, I would drop to my knees by her bed and pray. I did the same over my son's bed as I had always done. My heart was broken to know my children were heading down this road. I cried out to the Lord daily for them.

And then one day, totally unexpectedly, my daughter came and told me she wanted to serve the Lord. I was excited with the news! I could hardly believe my ears! This was my daughter standing in front of me saying she wanted to serve the Lord!

Parents, grandparents, keep praying for your prodigal children. He hears you when you pray and in the midst of the dark valley, He is working.

I can remember the excitement and thinking, she needs to get baptized now! I was overjoyed and was thanking the Lord. I was ready to tell her what her next step should be. I wanted to be the one to lead her where she had to go. But I felt the Lord stop me. I knew He didn't want me to say anything to her. He would lead and guide her. Amazingly, the following day, she asked me about baptism. She wanted to be baptized. I called my cousin Joy. Her husband was a pastor and we wanted to know if he could baptize her. She said she would get back to me. And before I knew it we were gathered around her waiting for her baptism. Derek and my cousin's husband both had the honor of submerging her into the water. And she came out with resurrection power. The whole thing was beautiful. What a day that was!

A few months later we found a farmhouse on the outskirts of Yorkton. It was a nice house with several acres of farmland. Behind the house were three old army barrack buildings. In the evening, when it was dark, my daughter would go for walks out there. I don't know how she ever did it because I couldn't bring myself to do the same. I found it creepy back there, but she would come in the back door and I knew she had been with Jesus. She loved going out there to worship and to have that time with Him out there. During the day, Derek and the boys and I would go for walks and we looked into those old barracks. And we could see that there was a lot of garbage in them which appeared to have been in there for years. From our perspective, nothing was salvageable in there.

One evening as I was sitting at the kitchen table Hasslina came in from one of her walks. She came in carrying books and put them on the table. As soon as I saw them I was surprised. Every book she put on the table were all Christian books and they were intact! She had gone into those barracks and found them. I felt the Lord speak to my heart several things about that. The first is that no matter how dark it is, or how bleak the circumstances look, He is always there in our midst. The second was that no matter where my children are He is with them and I don't need to be afraid for them. He has them in the palm of His hands. And lastly, our circumstances may look barren and dead but He can spring forth life from any place. I was encouraged that day for all our children. We had more prodigals that we were trusting the Lord to bring in and restore. We can't be with all our grown children, or to see them when we want to, but they are in our hearts. Our heart's desire is for each of them to make heaven their home.

Hasslina's love for the Lord grew and she wanted to go to Bible college. I told her about Summit International School of Ministry, the school founded by the late David Wilkerson. He was the man of God who founded Teen Challenge and preached on the streets to the nothings and the nobody's. He ministered to the prostitute and gang members. I knew all about feeling like nothing and a nobody – until Jesus came into my life and transformed it. It was a requirement for students who attended Summit that they had to put away social media and electronics for the entire two years of their studies. Would she go knowing that she would have to give up her phone and electronics for the duration of her school year? She said yes without any hesitation. We started the process of the school application and the paperwork.

We waited and waited to get an acceptance letter and we didn't get one in the set time that we were told to expect it. We got nervous about it, but lo and behold, the Lord waited to give her the acceptance letter – on her birthday! We all knew that this was His gift to her. Now it was time to prepare and get ready to see our daughter soar without us. The day came when we saw her board the plane and head off for Grantville, Pennsylvania.

A few days later, I took the boys for an afternoon walk. My phone rang and I saw that it was Hasslina. She was calling to tell us that she was being isolated because she had tested positive for COVID. I had been worried about this happening. And it happened. Fear wanted to hit me. She was so far away from home and there was nothing that I could do. The Lord reassured my heart though that she was in the best place, among people who would be praying for her. I sat down on the park bench and finished my call with her. She said she was doing OK and was feeling all right and wasn't too sick. The days following were rough for me as her mother because I couldn't be with her and she was in isolation alone. But she got through it with no problems. And even with this, Hasslina was now in the United States. She was attending Bible College and we couldn't be happier.

Keep praying, Mom and Dad. We can form our own ideas of how we think things should happen for our children or our spouses, but when it is God, He goes beyond our own thinking, and our understanding. His ways are higher than our ways. We don't know what the Lord is doing but when we pray and hold up His promises, He is faithful to His Word. We must know His Word.

We loved the house and the property, but there was a heap of problems with sewage with the house, and we were scrambling to find a place again. This was our second home with sewage problems. And I wondered if that was supposed to mirror something that was happening in our spiritual lives? If so, then we had a lot of junk to remove out of our house. And something was stinking.

Now thanks be unto God, which always causeth us to triumph in Christ, and maketh manifest the savour of his knowledge by us in every place. For we are unto God a sweet savour of Christ, in them that are saved, and in them that perish: To the one we are the savour of death unto death: and to the other the savour of life unto life. And who is sufficient for these things? (2 Corinthians 2:14-16)

The Lord desires that we would be like Him and that our light would shine before men and others. He wants us to have the sweet savor of His Son, Jesus Christ.

The problems with the house were forcing us to move back into Yorkton. I remember looking at all our moving boxes when we first moved in and thinking this house was temporary. Now we were leaving again. I was tired of constantly moving time after time. Why couldn't we just find a house and settle down, find a church, and rear our family like everyone else was doing? It seemed like we had a hard time fitting in anywhere as far as a church. We knew that many mixed native ceremonial traditions with Christianity. This is known as syncretism. This was an area that we knew we would not compromise and neither one of us ever did. Other churches were closely connected with my family in ministry and often followed their belief in the prosperity gospel which we did not agree with.

By this time we were well aware about a sickness that was coming from out of China. It had gotten the world's attention. We watched as COVID-19 hospitalized people and many others die from it. The mandates for vaccines were put into place and this was where we drew the line. We were not comfortable with putting anything into our body. It was our choice, our body, and our hope was in God. We respected the choice of others and held on to ours. Our jobs were dependent on us doing weekly COVID tests and we were not comfortable with that. We felt it wouldn't be long before the vaccine would no longer be a choice, but mandatory. We spoke about possibly even leaving Canada. We needed confirmation from the Lord and it came. I don't remember if it was a vision, or a dream, or both, but Derek saw that a darkness was coming across Canada, and we were to head south, across the border of Canada into the United States. Then one Sunday afternoon he watched an online church service and got confirmation again of going south.

With the decision to leave settled and confirmed, my concern shifted to our oldest son. He was an adult but we have always been close and with the way things were going, I did not want to leave him behind. But would he come? He had a girlfriend, would she come? I didn't know but the decision for us to go was made. I really began praying because I needed His grace and His strength for whatever was going to happen.

It was in my prayer time that the Lord reminded me of the story of Rahab. She believed God would save her and her family. When the Israelite spies came to Jericho she knew that God was going to destroy Jericho. She hid the spies in her home and asked them to spare her life and her family's lives when God destroyed Jericho. They agreed and asked her to hang a scarlet red rope from her window so that she would be saved at the appointed time. As I cried out to the Lord in prayer for my son the Lord spoke this word to my heart, "Not one will be left behind." I knew the Lord was giving me His promise. I was encouraged. Our son was not going to be left behind. I told my husband about this and he suggested I go to the store and buy a red sash to remember His promise. He wanted to hang it up on our door like Rahab did. I agreed, but each time I went, I would forget. It was on my heart to do so but the Lord had other plans.

It was getting close to our departure date and we still had no idea if our son would be coming. Derek came home from work one day and asked me to go for a walk. The uncertainty of what laid ahead was very heavy on us all. We needed to get out and spend some time together and with the Lord. We drove down to the Gallagher Center, a recreational facility in the community. It had a beautiful nature path behind it.

When we got there it felt like Derek and I were the only ones there. It was nice and I needed the walk. As we came around one particular bend on the pathway, I saw something red ahead in one of the bushes. I was shocked to see that it was a long sash-like red rope hanging in a bush directly in front of us! Immediately, the story of Rahab and the words I'd heard "Not one will be left behind!" came to my mind. I moved quickly over to the tree it was hanging on, and I grabbed it! This was unbelievable. But yet, there it was. Derek and I looked at each other. How could this even be possible? But there it was and we knew He was making it known to us both that He was in our midst. He was concerned with all that we had in our heart. This was one of those moments that will always be a clear reminder to us of our wonderful heavenly Father. This was our Red Sea moment. This was His promise to us.

My mom and my sisters lived on Key First Nation at the time and I told her what we were planning to do. She also saw the events unfolding around us and that our world was quickly changing. It wasn't long before she decided that she would be coming with us as well. That was it, it was settled. We were all crossing over. It didn't come without some backlash though and some hurt feelings. It was hard because this was our home and some of our family members didn't like it. We knew that many didn't understand what we were doing. There was no middle ground and with the mandates in place we began to see the division of family members. It sliced households in half and it was dividing us from our family and friends. My husband had daughters in the north, we had grandchildren and family there too. But we knew we had to go and the Lord had shown and confirmed it to us three times. How long would we be gone for? We didn't know.

We packed up and headed south. We were concerned with the border because we had read how it was locked down due to COVID. No one could come or go. We traveled in three vehicles. My mother, my sisters and my son's girlfriend were with her in her van, and we had our two vehicles. Derek drove with Hassan, and I went with the boys in our other vehicle. And it happened as the Lord said it would. We made it over the border. When the boys and I crossed over Derek and Hassan were waiting for us on the side of the road. When we pulled over to meet them, I went up to see Hassan and gave him a big hug and held out that red string to him and placed it in his hand. I reminded him of the Lord's promise to me, *"Not one will be left behind."*

Before we left Canada, we were driving down Main Street in Yorkton and passed by a park that we passed all the time. But on that day when I looked over at the park, it stood out, and I envisioned us singing and setting up a table for my books. And that's exactly what we did a few weeks later. We set up a table and a small sound system. Derek played some worship music and we sang. It was a beautiful day. We had a few people come here and there but it didn't get busy. We will always remember a young native couple that came to the front of the small park stage. I approached them and talked to them. Their hearts were being touched. Then we saw another man sitting behind the stage. As Derek was singing, he had been crying. That really spoke to me of the hunger and thirst that people have for the Lord in this time. I was waiting for a friend named Doreen to come by who I had known from Facebook. She messaged and asked me what time I was going to be there at the park. She came that afternoon to meet me and she brought a gift for me. I was so surprised by that. It was a glass frame that held a beautiful display of art that she had crafted from rocks. She had them form a letter "I". One of the rocks was in the shape of a heart. At the bottom of the frame there was a quote from my book *Rise Up My Beloved*. It simply read "You're only passing through. -Jesus"

It blessed my heart so much. It was a bittersweet moment because being back in my home province came with more pain. I pushed through and tried to reconcile with my family by going to church functions and their dinners but there was no reconciling. But seeing my gift was a reminder that I am only passing through. I may not have been received, but He has people that will love and take me in. Another sister, who I had never met before and was only passing through, came to our table and bought ten books from me. She came back later to order even more.

I didn't have much when I left Canada but I made sure that I brought my rock art from Doreen with me. It is a gift that is very precious to me. I will keep it with me, always.

Derek

When COVID hit the world, my wife and I could see that Canada was headed in a direction we did not like. We sought the Lord about it and through three different ways – a vision, a dream, and a message – He told us to go south. And so in October 2020, we packed up everything we could in our minivan and small SUV and headed south. My mother-in-law decided that she would also come. After four days of travel we ended up in Harrisburg, Pennsylvania. It was just a half hour away from where our daughter was in Bible College.

The next three months were a time of great stretching in all of us, but especially in me. This was the first time that I had ever been without work since I had started working as a young man. And it wasn't for lack of trying. I applied to hundreds of jobs, but I found nothing. My mother-in-law found a job in a local Christian organization. The money we had soon ran out and our church and the organizations that had been helping said they would no longer help us. And in the middle of it all, my wife and I caught COVID. My wife lost her sense of taste and smell (and has yet to regain them). I ended up in the hospital where I almost lost my life. But the Lord kept me. During this time I learned to sing even in the midst of my suffering. I learned I could trust Him when faced with great fear. He was teaching me through this time. And I was trying my best to be a studious student. But I had much to unlearn. Religion had choked out the work of the Spirit of God in my life. Up until this time, it had been me doing the "work" and I had been in the way of allowing the Lord to work in my life. This was a time of pressing and pruning to get Derek out of the way.

Without work, my wife and I prayed. Joined by my mother-in-law we prayed and asked the Lord what to do. I truly believed that He told us to go. We took the little money we had left and began heading "south" toward Arizona. What we would find there, we had no idea. We said good-bye to my mother-in-law and headed off to wherever the Lord would lead us.

We left Pennsylvania and traveled south through Virginia, Kentucky, Tennessee, Oklahoma, Texas, New Mexico, and finally came to Arizona. Along every mile of the way, God kept us. Not once did we ever go hungry, not once did we ever go without shelter. In fact, we had some friends who watched our journey on social media ask us if we had won the lottery! We had two vehicles to fuel, two rooms to cover each night and God faithfully kept us through it all. It was the most trying and humbling time of my life.

There were many moments of crying out to God during this time. And there were also many moments where God showed His faithfulness. In these times of pressing you find out what is really in your heart. And anger, unbelief, fear, and doubt hit me hard. Very hard. It didn't just bubble to the surface. It flowed out like a ferocious boiling pot of water! And to see what I had in my heart was hard to face. Pride and religion wanted to deny it. But the evidence was there. And yet, through it all, the Lord was showing me His faithfulness.

After seeing the Grand Canyon, we left Arizona and started heading back East. Although somewhat discouraged by the seemingly fruitlessness of our trip, we knew God was still somehow at work and guiding us every step. We had a brief stop in New Mexico and then we found ourselves in Oklahoma. It was here that the Lord would put us through the most trying time of our entire trip.

But it was also a time when I had my most profound moment with the Lord.

My wife reached out to a friend we had met some years ago in Toronto, ON. She was now studying and living in Tulsa, OK. She offered up her one-bedroom apartment for us to stay in while we did what we could to begin a new life in Tulsa. We spent about two weeks in that small apartment. But it was here, on a Saturday morning in February, that my wife and I over coffee and breakfast began sharing what the Lord had been doing and had done for us during the past month. We both could see that the Lord had been breaking down my religious and hardened heart. We talked about His goodness and His love as we studied His Word together. Our host had spent the night out and we had the breakfast table to ourselves. It was here that the Lord spoke to me, through His Word, something so profound that it literally changed my life.

I had never fully recognized my religious state. I didn't want to admit to what I felt was ridiculous. I was proud and arrogant about my "walk" with Christ. I was so blinded by my pride that I failed – and refused – to see that I was religious. My wife would point it out to me time and time again, and each time I would get angry and defensive. Who was she to tell me what kind of Christian I was? Who did she think she was? Was she somehow better than me? These were thoughts that would invade my mind each time she would say something to me about being religious. And it would make me more and more bitter. But the Lord had brought her into my life to bring me out of it. And in order to do so, He had to crush and break me to bring me to my knees and to open my blinded eyes. And His way is always the best way.

As I sat and read the second chapter of John, I came to verse 48. The words of Jesus hit me: "When thou wast under the fig tree, I saw thee." To fully describe the depth at which I felt those words is impossible. But I felt those words hit something inside of me that shook me. I knew He was speaking directly to me at that very moment. I read the words back to my wife. As I did, they reverberated in my spirit so powerfully that I immediately began shaking and crying. I was overwhelmed by the reality I was faced with. I had been a religious man and I was now seeing it clearly for the first time. And yet, in my religious pride and arrogance, He saw me and wanted to be with me. He saw me and He loved me. He saw me under that cursed fig tree of religion.

The Lord had been using this time of great pressing and crushing to bring me to this very place. It was time for me to look in the mirror placed in front of me.

The hand of the Lord moved mightily in that time. More testing came and my faith and trust in Him were pushed to my limits once again. After almost two months on the road, we decided it was time to head back to Pennsylvania. Through the hand of a beloved couple in the Lord, we were blessed with enough money to make the trip back.

I don't remember much of the trip back. All I remember is that we decided we would head to Butler, PA, a small town approximately 45 minutes north of Pittsburgh, PA. It was March 2021 and once again, we were in a strange town with nowhere to go and no job. We called the social assistance hotline and we were referred to a homeless agency. And for the next month and a half, we lived under their auspices. Even here, the Lord continued working on me. The agency had an "employment counselor" who I found to be very uncouth and very mean-spirited. Through him, the Lord continued breaking off the religious arrogance and pride in my heart.

One day, during our daily "check-in" appointments, he and I had a shouting match that left me very angry and upset. My heart wanted to rush toward malicious intent. I was so angry. That evening, the Lord showed me that He had placed this man in our path to be a blessing to our family. He had put him in that place to help my family in time of need. The very next day, I went to see him, and although I wanted nothing more than to get back at him, the Lord chastened my heart in that moment, and I humbly apologized. Whether it was he or I that were at fault did not matter, I did not want my heart to be overcome with malice. I knew that the Lord had given me the opportunity to be humble and to submit myself to this man. After a month and a half in this "shelter," the Lord moved. After moving to the US and being homeless and jobless for six months, the Lord blessed me with two jobs and our own place. It was small, but it was our own place. And we loved it! But most importantly, He had done an incredible work of transformation in my heart during this time.

Our daughter completed her first year of Bible College about a month later and came to live with us that summer. When she went back to Bible College, about 4.5 hours away from Butler, we felt her absence and desired to be closer to her, and to my mother-in-law who was living in Harrisburg, PA, just a 30-minute drive from our daughter's Bible College. I started looking for work in Harrisburg and the Lord opened the door for an interview with a men's Christian homeless shelter. After having spent time in a shelter ourselves, I knew what someone could expect when coming into a shelter. I knew that above all, I wanted to treat those coming to the shelter with dignity, because there had been so many times in our journey when we were treated with such a degree of disdain and disrespect it had hurt and wounded us. But despite it all, we knew that the Lord was using it for His glory. When I spoke this same thought to the Director of the Men's Mission, he immediately knew he wanted to hire me. I later learned that when he had accepted his position as Director he had written a vision statement of how he wanted to see the mission run. And one of his goals was to have the men treated with dignity. It was the Lord who had made this possible. I

would have never spoken those words unless the Lord had taken me
through our own homeless journey.

Thirteen

COVID

We headed south across the border and began a four-day journey to Pennsylvania. Just before we got into Pennsylvania, as we drove through the rolling hills we encountered a bad rainstorm. The rain became so bad that the vehicle Derek was driving began to hydroplane and they almost ran off the road. It was a scary moment because the vehicle had four bad tires. Derek later said that he cried out to Jesus and they straightened out almost immediately.

As we continued to drive, Derek told me later how that at the same moment they saw the sign for the state of Pennsylvania, the skies began to clear and a beautiful rainbow filled the sky ahead of them. I had always told my children Bible stories and Hassan knew the story of Noah. Seeing the rainbow hit Hassan, as he remembered the promise before we left Canada that not one would be left behind. It was as if God was reminding us all, and especially Hassan, of how we all had made it safely and how He would continue to hold us all.

A few hours later we pulled right up to Hasslina's school. What a sight we must have been! We had three "rezzed-out" vehicles which included my mother's van towing a rusty half pick-up truck trailer. If it was me watching this caravan roll in, I would have thought, "Who are these people driving up 'Rez-style' on this proper campus?" I can imagine that Hasslina was happy to see us, and yet probably slightly embarrassed at the same time. But all of us were extremely glad to have made it and to see her!

After meeting with Hasslina, we didn't know where we were going next. We found a cheap motel on Front Street in Harrisburg. Derek made some phone calls over the next few days. He was able to get us some financial assistance and secure our Social Security numbers which also meant we would have Medicaid. This turned out to be the Lord's doing as we did not know that we would soon need it.

Our motel room was situated by a river. It was beautiful, and we had a view of the Blue Mountains and the Susquehanna River. We started to walk the path along the river every day. I was still walking the *100 Days Walking By Faith* journey and sharing online. Derek started walking with the boys everyday too. He was up to walking an hour each day. I was happy that he was focusing on keeping his health. I was buying vitamins and making sure we were taking them everyday. We were avoiding the inevitable and hoping that we would not catch COVID.

Then it happened. We got hit by COVID. I had taken all the necessary precautions and made sure we all sanitized our hands anytime we went out anywhere. The only place I went was Walmart.

One afternoon, I began to have a headache and sore throat. The following day, I had an intense ache in my face. It felt like I had been hit in the jaw. Derek started to suspect I had it once I told him my symptoms. He looked concerned and went and picked up a rapid test and our fears were confirmed. I had COVID. I moved down to my son's room a few doors down to protect my boys. That didn't matter because on day five of my isolation, my husband said he was coming down with a sore throat. He took a home test and also tested positive for COVID. I moved back to our room because it made no sense being apart since we both now had COVID. All we could do was wait it out.

Our boys began having symptoms at the same time but they sailed through with no problems. I had the worst sinus congestion of my life but I was managing. We were counting the days and anxious to get past day eight because that seemed to be the day that determined if somebody needed to go to the hospital, or if it was going to pass. I went to the ER on day eight because I was still getting fevers and my head hurt so bad and the doctor told me that I had to let it run its course.

When Derek got to day seven he was sounding more congested. The following morning, I felt him pat me on the back and he said, "We have to go to the ER," and my heart sank. I could see from the night before that he was having a harder time breathing. It was taking a lot for him just to walk to the washroom. But before leaving that morning, he posted on social media that we were on our way to the hospital and was asking for prayer. A brother in the Lord commented on his post, "Don't let anyone give you Remdesivir." When we got to the ER they had to put him on high oxygen right away. He had to use a wheelchair because he didn't have the strength to stand. He couldn't breathe any longer on his own and the doctor said that he had respiratory failure. The thing I feared most was happening. And my husband had no strength in him. He was so frail and weak. I felt the very ground rip out from underneath me. It was the scariest time of my life with the thought of losing my husband. I had to push the doubts and thoughts out of my head about him never coming home to me again. We had heard the news and saw how people went into the hospital after their health declined because they had to go on ventilators. I had to trust the Lord with all I had, what else did I have?

I went and picked up a bristle board from the dollar tree and wrote healing scriptures on it and began praying. The torment and the fears I had came from every direction. I had to believe that we didn't come all this way for me to become a widow while living in a motel. I called my friend Norma back in Ontario and she prayed for me. I don't remember much of the conversation but what I can recall was her telling me that I needed to get up and start praying! I felt like a mighty warrior who was surrounded by enemies and I had to fight! I was strengthened and encouraged. We had a friend Becky from Canada who knew someone from around Harrisburg. She reached out to him and he would come out to the motel to drop off money and food. He prayed with me for my family. Our church brought food and medicine for us. When we were at our lowest the Lord sent in His people. I will remember that for the rest of my life.

In front of the motel where we stayed is a hill. One day as I was looking out of my motel window after being in prayer, the Lord spoke to me that He was going to bring my family through. He was going to make a pathway for us to walk through this mountain that was in front of us and lead us out. I had heard an exhortation weeks before about mountains being moved and brought down, and it came flooding back to me. He would give us a testimony. The most incredible part of this journey was that while my husband was in the hospital with COVID, he was singing.

Even while in the Emergency dept., he went live on Facebook to sing. He did this everyday. He would share and sing a praise and worship song to the Lord. And the people were encouraged and were blessed by this. I cried watching and marveled at the goodness of God. My husband was alive and singing! He never quit or gave up hope but kept running to the Lord. He even had episodes of panic attacks that would hit him. He described feeling intense fear, wanting to rip off the oxygen and flee the hospital, but he knew he couldn't do that or he would die. But the Lord would use that to draw Derek closer to Him. His birthday came and went. The hospital wouldn't let me go and see him and that was the hardest part. All I wanted to do was kiss my husband and hold him. I wanted to hug him so badly. We were texting and I was seeing him on his live videos but it wasn't the same. The Lord remained faithful. We did not get consumed and He brought us through. After seven days of being in the hospital he came home. He had to carry oxygen with him all the time and it was still difficult to go to the bathroom and walk around because everything took his breath away. It was gradual but he regained his strength.

Derek later told me that while he was in the emergency department, he was so tired and wanted to sleep. But he would be awakened by something. In one instance, we knew the Lord had kept him awake for a purpose. When Derek had posted that he was going into the ER, a friend had told him not to take Remdisivir. But it was at one moment when he had been sleeping that the alarm beeping from the IV woke him up. Just as he woke up a nurse came in with an IV bag and some medication. Years before, Derek had worked in a hospital and so he recognized that they were about to give him some medicine through the IV line. Derek asked, "What is that?" The nurse told him that it was Remdisivir. Derek got upset and told them, "I don't want that!" The doctor had ordered the medication without ever meeting Derek and speaking to him about it. We found out later how many people had been badly affected by this drug. We thank the Lord for that friend who warned us beforehand.

We had our Christmas in the motel but it was good. We contacted the Salvation Army and a couple of places for help with Christmas. The boys were not disappointed. They received a lot of gifts. Their faces were filled with smiles and we all enjoyed a happy Christmas in that little motel room.

Soon, it came time for us to leave again. The job Derek had applied for didn't come through and we had no money to stay another month. We had no choice but to leave and hit the road again. We packed up our belongings and crammed four adults, our two boys and three pets into our two vehicles. Off we went. We had no real destination, but we had to trust the Lord to lead us for a job and a place to live. We traveled from Pennsylvania and headed for southwestern USA. We drove through several states including Arkansas, Texas, Oklahoma, New Mexico, and finally came to Arizona. There were so many instances of God's provision on our journey.

Our first stop was to meet a brother in the Lord who was a friend of Derek. He gave us a room in Kentucky. I think we will always remember that place because it was situated on a steep hill. It was raining when we arrived, and we drove up a winding road that led to the top of a high hill. The motel had a beautiful scenic view overlooking the town. It was incredible. The following morning we took off again.

There was one point that we didn't know where we were going to get our next tank of gas from and it was looking pretty rough. My husband had said that if he had to, he'd play guitar and sing. As we stood there in that parking lot of the truck stop, Derek went to unload the guitar, walked over to the front of the truck stop, and started playing guitar and singing! Here we were, on a journey where we had no idea where we were going, except for a word from the Lord to go south, no money and almost out of gas, and my husband was standing in front of a Loves truck stop singing and playing guitar. I was beside myself in tears laughing at our situation. The crazy thing is that people started to give and he made enough money to put a tank of gas in our vehicles. We were back on the road again.

We found our way to Williams, Arizona where we got a room and decided on finding a church. We attended a service at a small church and got a chance to speak to the pastor and told him about our situation. We gave him one of my books and he helped pay for our rooms for the week. We were so thankful to the Lord for that because he covered our two rooms. When nothing came up for jobs or opportunities, we headed toward Oklahoma.

I went live on Facebook and a woman who had been following me on Facebook reached out and blessed us with a small apartment for three nights. She wanted to meet me and gave us a place to stay for the weekend. This was in Santa Fe, New Mexico. It was here that we went to a native friendship center.

When we went inside and we started to talk about where we were from, we found out that the young girl who was working there was from my home reserve back in Canada. She had called her mom and told her about us and the following day she told me that her mother wanted to take us out for breakfast at IHOP. It was so funny because we had seen IHOP restaurants everywhere along our trip and we wanted to go there. We were finally eating at IHOP and our boys loved it! We still laugh about it to this day, because when our son's pancakes came, he thought they had placed whipped cream on his pancakes, but instead it was a big ball of butter that he put into his mouth! When it came time to leave she wanted us to come to her vehicle because she had something for us. She handed us several bags of food and two Queen sized blankets. We were so incredibly blessed!

We had some friends who lived in Tulsa, OK. We were offered a place to sleep in their homes. We stayed in Tulsa for about a month or so. On our way through we had a friend from Facebook that neither of us knew, but she was from Canada. Her name was Cindy and she invited us to come stay at her place. She welcomed us and we camped in her living room. What a beautiful friend we met in

Tulsa. I don't think I'll ever forget her hospitality and the love that she gave to me and my family. Although we tried our best to settle in Tulsa nothing worked out for us. But she and her family were an incredible blessing to us!

One day my husband and I were reading our Word together at the kitchen table. The Lord spoke to him about when Nathaniel was underneath the fig tree. Andrew went to call him and Jesus said to him, "Nathaniel, when you were under the fig tree, I saw you." It hit my husband's heart; the Lord saw him. He had been under there all those years but the Lord had seen him. God was definitely doing something new because my husband could never see where he was before. The Lord was showing him where he was and the things in his heart.

We went as far as Arizona and our stopover there was interesting, to say the least. When we pulled into Phoenix, Arizona, our hope was to find a motel because we had been on the road all day. It was around midnight. The kids were tired and our pets needed food. They were good travelers though and we were thankful for that. Nikki loved vehicle rides. She always knew when we were getting ready to leave. One click on her leash and she came running. She knew the drill and she loved it. But by the end of the day she wanted to get out.

We needed gas and found a gas station which seemed busy with a lot of people and activity. The boys and I ran in to use the bathroom while Derek fueled up our two vehicles. I held onto my son's hands so they wouldn't run ahead of me. I didn't usually hold their hands but with the amount of activity around the place, I held on to them. As we came out of the store, a truck and two police cruisers came speeding into the parking lot. We were almost hit by one of the police cruisers. The police cruisers pulled up to corner a truck sitting in front of the store. One cruiser beside it and another behind it. It all happened so fast. With the boys' hands firmly in mine, I quickly picked up my pace trying to get to where Derek was filling up the vehicle. I didn't see Derek right away because he was a few feet from the vehicle watching cruisers on the other side of the street. There was a street fight going on. The whole scene was bizarre.

A day or two later, Hassan told us that the spot we had rolled into had been highlighted on a Netflix documentary as one of America's most dangerous neighborhoods.

There is a quote from Billy Graham that safety is not in the absence of danger, but in the presence of the Lord. There can be things happening on all sides of you and danger lurking on every corner, but if the Lord's hand is upon you then you are in safety.

We paid for a room at a motel, but changed our minds quickly when we stepped inside. I have been in some dingy rounds before, but this one topped the charts! It had half a headboard and the other half of it was knocked out. The cockroaches were visible on the walls. I could have probably handled a few roaches, but the parties and strip clubs beside us had us back in the vehicle. That was it for our money and our refund would take a couple of days. We decided to leave. I remember seeing camping trailers and other vehicles parked out in Walmart parking lots before. Why couldn't we do that? I googled it and found that it was ok for us to park there. We ended up staying that night in a Walmart parking lot. The sleep was rough but thankfully, we got enough rest.

I remember waking up and seeing a cactus in front of our vehicle the following morning. They lined the parking lot and they were beautiful. I had never seen real cactus before, much less wake up to them with music in the background. Walmart played music and it could be heard throughout the whole lot.

We spent a week in Arizona as we checked out the local native agencies but found no immediate employment opportunities. The emergency housing list was long. Masking and vaccine mandates were in place and we knew it was time for us to head back towards

Pennsylvania. Regardless of what happened, the whole trip was amazing. We didn't know where we would sleep but the Lord made a way for us. We made some new friends along the way. We saw the hand of God move and provide for us. It was truly miraculous. It was learning to walk in faith.

We met up with another friend, our brother, in the Lord, who had interviewed me in the past for my book, *Rise Up My Beloved*. We have been online friends through the years, but had never met. We let him know that we were coming through Tulsa and he asked us to meet him somewhere. When we got to the address, he treated all of us to supper. And then, he and his wife paid for two rooms for us for a couple of nights. Their giving and generosity greatly encouraged us. God has His people everywhere.

We had one moment, however, that has been firmly etched into our memory. It came when we first arrived in Tulsa. We were needing some help and as we were driving around we saw a church with a sign that seemed to indicate it was a church that not only had the financial means to help, but also the willingness to go beyond. The church was glamorous and it was huge! We pulled into the parking lot and went in. Someone approached us and we told them what we needed and asked if the pastor was available. They left and when they came back they were led by someone. We found out that he was not the pastor but some other leader. We were embarrassed when he told us to call 211 which is a social services helpline. We left feeling very discouraged, but I felt the Lord come and stir my heart. He spoke to me that 'Not everyone is like this,' and that He was going to look after us. I felt the Lord's strength and His grace upon us. I knew the Lord was going deep into Derek's heart. Being the husband, father and provider this was heavy on Derek.

We continued on with our journey back to Pennsylvania and finally settled in Butler, Pennsylvania. We had lived in motels from October to April and we finally found a two-story house to rent that could accommodate us all. Hassan and his girlfriend rented the downstairs apartment and we took the upstairs apartment.

The top of the apartment had a huge space upstairs that we gave to our daughter Hasslina. When she went back to school, I took refuge up there. And it was my prayer spot.

I had one time in prayer with the Lord that I will remember because it was such a heavenly moment. I was worshiping to the song, "*Wait On The Lord*" and His presence was very strong. I knew He was saying, "*Just wait, wait on Me.*" There were good things coming. There were many times I wanted to run away. I wanted to scream and get angry that things were so hard. But what would that do? I'd been in that place of frustration and I can attest that no amount of jumping or screaming changes anything. I had to surrender everything to the Lord. And He would give the grace to get through.

Derek took a limo job and we did food delivery. That was good for a while but it was a lot of long hours and he had to be on call. That was proving to be difficult when he had to be on the road at 2:00 AM. He began to look in Harrisburg for work. We wanted to be closer to my mom. Then he got the job at the Men's Mission in Harrisburg. It was a four-hour drive from Butler to Harrisburg, so commuting daily was not an option. The plan was for him to stay with my mom in Harrisburg. He would work Monday to Friday and come back home on weekends. Most times he would take a bus. Sometimes, I would drive him down to Harrisburg. It was a rough time. About a month after he started working at the Men's Mission, Derek caught COVID again and he was very sick. The last time he was sick was still fresh in my memory and I knew I had to see him. I drove down to Harrisburg and picked him up. We came home and I took care of him by placing an onion poultice on his chest. I would then have him lay face down on the bed to "drum" on his back. This helped to loosen up the phlegm in his lungs. He got back to work after a few days. The Lord was keeping him strong.

After a couple of months we found our own place in Harrisburg. We moved into an apartment. It was big enough for all of us but it came with Harrisburg's creakiest floors. I mean anytime Derek used the bathroom, he woke me up. There was no sneaking to the kitchen for late snacks. We still had Nikki but because of the floors, Nikki lost her place to sleep in our room. I have always been a light sleeper. When she would come into our room, she made the floors creak and it always woke me up at night. I've gotten used to the snoring now, but with Derek's sleep apnea, getting a good night's sleep for me has been rough. But even with the creaky floors, it was home and we had much to be thankful for. When Christmas came around again we had a beautiful tree with all the decorations and lights. It was a beautiful Christmas.

Fourteen

Bethesda

The Bethesda Men's Mission is located in the central part of
Harrisburg, Pennsylvania. This was where Derek found work. It
would not have been his first choice but he really didn't have any
other options. Every other job that came his way involved him traveling on the road at all hours of the night. That was not something
we wanted to do. Derek didn't like leaving us and I didn't like the
thought of that either.

I hadn't put much thought into the meaning of "Bethesda" until
very recently. The Lord kept bringing it to me. He would bring me
to the story of the lame man at Bethesda time and time again. It
was either through the course we were taking or through sermons I
listened to. What I didn't know was that it would be a part of our
story that would turn into a message. When I decided to look it up
in the Bible, I was surprised to see that its chapter referenced our
number fifteen. I am still amazed by this.

The name Bethesda in Hebrew means "a house of mercy" or "a
house of grace." It is a covering for those who need healing. Through

this I believe the Lord is saying "It doesn't matter what you have done, I will take you up and receive you as my own."

In John 5:15 we read of a man who had been lame for 38 years. He would go down to a pool named Bethesda. It was there that an angel would go at a certain time to stir the waters. When that happened the first person who entered the water would get healed. Jesus came to the pool and saw the man. He asked him, "Do you want to be made whole?" He told Jesus that whenever he attempted to go down into the water another would step in front of him. Jesus instructed the man, "Get up and take up your bed and walk." And he was healed on that day.

There are 100 beds at the Bethesda Men's Mission. Men go there seeking refuge and a place to sleep. Most struggle with addictions and mental health. They are homeless and go there in hopes of finding shelter and safety. They have become lame in the sense that they have lost their way, and, in some cases, have given up hope.

Bethesda is a symbolic place for all to come down to the water for healing. And in a sense, if we would only be honest, we're all lame. We're all struggling in some area of our lives. You may not be homeless or may not have an addiction but there is a struggle, a pain, or some kind of infirmity that you're tired of carrying around.

It was not a coincidence that the place my husband was called to work would be the place that the Lord would deliver and set him free at.

Derek had difficulty working at the mission as a House Supervisor when he started. It's a hard place to work. There is a lot to contend with at a homeless shelter. He completes the intakes and he monitors the cameras. It's a demanding job and one with few breaks. He called me one day in frustration, "I can't deal with these kids!!" He was upset and he was ready to walk out of there. And he would have, had he had another option. He liked the men that worked there. They were "down to earth." They weren't polished but they looked to the Lord. They saw how the Lord provided for the mission. The Bethesda Men's Mission has been there for 100 years. And history has shown that the Lord provides miracles there in the hearts and lives of the men that come through there. My husband would not be the first.

He had several days and weeks of feeling like he wanted to walk out. But we knew without a doubt that the Lord had called him there. His salary was the lowest he had ever received. He didn't make enough to cover all the bills and I knew he was having a hard time with not being able to provide for his family. We were barely making it from paycheck to paycheck. We had to use government assistance and food stamps. But we knew we had to stay where He placed us because the Lord was at work. Anytime that we tried to look for other work or go in another direction, it didn't feel right. It felt like we were fighting against the Lord's will. We continued to stay on and the Lord met all our needs. It was rough at times and it felt like we were calves stuck in a stall, waiting to be released. We didn't have the money to keep ourselves busy with other activities or to take trips. Instead, the Lord used this time to bring things within our hearts to the surface. It was pruning time.

Derek's pruning place was work. Mine was at home. I was busy writing this book, homeschooling, and online ministry. I was serving my family, taking an online course to get my counseling certificate, and we had completed two *In Christ Image* training certificates by *Francis Frangipane Ministries*. And then, I also started working part-time at the Bethesda Women's Mission.

I hold a packed full-time schedule and I can attest to you that none of this would be possible if not by the grace of God. The pruning process would be hard but necessary. I would learn more of His character about how giving and loving He is. The Word describes God as omnipotent, which means He is all powerful and when He moves and performs His miracles, He doesn't lose His power. He is omniscient, meaning all-knowing and He knows all things. He knows how all things will be and how it will all end. But yet, He is still present with us now in our times of need.

He is omnipresent, meaning present everywhere at all times. He is a God who is everywhere all at the same time. He is here with me now and with you right now.

I used to struggle with being a stay-at-home mom. At different times I resented it, but now I see that it's an honor and privilege to stay home and rear my children. And to see the times we live in now, I see His mercy and grace upon our home. Serving my husband and my children are my first ministry. One day they will launch off on their own and they need to be ready for the things they will face. We need to prepare our children for the days ahead. This was my responsibility as a mom. And I held this title with great joy.

The Lord spoke to my heart that I could not just tell my children to pray and believe in God, I needed to demonstrate it in how I lived my life for him. What I mean by this is showing our children how to pray and how to live out our Christian lives out loud. We can't assume that our children know how to pray because we tell them to. Without our instruction, they will struggle with how to open up and bare their hearts. The Lord spoke to my heart to pray in front of them. And that's what I now do; I pray in front of them as I would in my secret closet. I want them to know and understand that they can pour out their heart the things that bother them, their worries, and their fears. The boys and I come together in our living room and the three of us will get down on our knees and we take turns praying to the Lord. The other day, while my husband was sick and stayed home from work, I turned and saw him kneeling too. I didn't realize that he was there with us.

Then, after our prayer time, I will share from our devotions. I expound on it so it's clear to them and they usually have questions. The Lord always stirs and moves our hearts. As I served and loved my family it determined the kind of fruit I would bear. I began to take the calling of "mom" more seriously. My children were my greatest blessings and I was given this honor to steward what He placed in my hands. The Lord is first in my life. From Him comes all good things that allow me to serve my husband and my children. I try to lead by example in every facet of my life and I point my family to Jesus. Do I mess up? Of course, everyday. But I point them to the Lord. And I have explained to them that we don't put any confidence in anyone. We all fall short but the Lord never will. And if our children know this powerful truth, they will always know where to run to. It is our hope that we go from glory to glory and become more Christ-like in our lives and how we live.

But we all, with open face beholding as in a glass the glory of the Lord, are changed into the same image from glory to glory, even as by the Spirit of the Lord. (2 Corinthians 3:18)

We are living in perilous times. But those who place their hope in the Lord will shine brightly. And we have to use every day to prepare our hearts to meet Him. We won't make the coming days without Him. I've been walking with the Lord for 23 years now and He is still my everything. I will not be a casual or lukewarm Christian. I will not do things halfway, or be nonchalant, and I do not want my children to be either.

As I yielded more to the Holy Spirit I saw much fruit in my home and in me. I had a hunger and passion in my heart for truth. I had a fire in me and nothing was going to hinder that.

My husband and I no longer argued as much, and there wasn't any more yelling in our home. The yelling was a big factor in our home and the Lord showed me how damaging it was one day. I'm not sure the reason why my husband was upset with one of the boys but, like he often did, he yelled at one of them. But when he did it this time, his voice went right through me. It shook me to the core and I realized then how much that could affect our boys. And it broke my heart that we had been so blind before. I didn't see anything wrong with yelling before that point because he wasn't spanking them or abusing them. But by the grace of God He shed light on that and I knew that it all had to stop.

Our boys belong to the Lord and we would answer to Him on how we rear them. We had to show them love in the same way He showed us love. And He is a tender loving Father. He is gentle and compassionate, slow to anger (Psalm 103:8). He doesn't yell at us but gently corrects us. God was moving in our home. His Word was working in the midst of us. He was bringing to light things that needed to change in our home. He was working all things out for our good.

I homeschool our boys and I have for several years now. While we lived in London they attended a Christian school. They have a friend they still remain in contact with from there. We were thankful for the time that they had in that school. But since so much has changed in our world we decided on homeschooling.

I have the boys read devotions every morning before they start their schoolwork. I have them write out what the Lord speaks to them each day during their devotion. As they read and the word goes deeper into their heart, other things have begun to surface. They started to share their struggles. In some measure or another my husband and I had hurt our sons from our own hurt and wounds we both carried. I spent too much time away from them because of school or from working too much on online ministry. And my husband was too hard on them at times. That was something that the Lord was changing all the time as the days went by. It was as though all our hearts were being healed during this time. He was our Heavenly Father and He saw things in our lives we didn't even know were there. He was at work in the midst and He was uprooting and pulling down strongholds and enemies that were in the shadows. The Lord heals our wounds so that we don't become hardened in our hearts. If our wounds don't heal, they will stay there and fester and nothing good comes from that. The enemy will use that wound to draw us into darker places. Places where we don't want to be.

> *But thou, O LORD, art a shield for me; my glory, and the lifter up of mine head. (Psalm 3:3)*

The Lord heals and sets us free. When we turn to the Lord everything changes. But sin will weigh us down.

As a little boy Derek knew that sin weighs you down. He told me a story of when he was a little boy. He told his uncle Herbert that the reason why Jesus could walk on water was because He had no sin. And the reason why his uncle couldn't walk on water was because he was full of sin. It was a short time afterward that his uncle Herbert went over to his parents' place. He told them 'because of what that little boy said to me, I want to give my life to Jesus.' This was the first person that Derek had led to the Lord.

We are but pieces of clay in the potter's hand. And to those who yield to Him resurrection power is given. My husband and I both desired for the presence of the Lord and long for the day we will see Him. The days of going to work didn't seem as hard for my husband. He was putting one foot in front of the other just as the Lord had spoken to him about years before on the side of the road. He may have known the word of the Lord most of his life but he had not come to the knowledge of the truth of who he was in the Lord (Ephesians 4:21). There are many in the same situation and they struggle with their walk. They know the word but it is not piercing into the heart. Like my dream about the man they called "The Walking Bible", he knew the word but it no longer convicted him and it had no power over him anymore. They deny the power of it by not drawing closer to the Lord. There is no true repentance, and no sorrow over their sin. Their hearts have become dull and cold.

"I believe in God but I can't believe that He loves me. Why would he want me? I'm worthless and no good! I wanna die!"

The condemnation that came upon Derek was heavy. He beat himself up continually and believed that I and the boys would be better off without him. Sometimes fear would come and make me wonder if I would come home to find that he had taken his life. But I knew the Lord showed me that he had a great calling on his life.

It was so hard to hear him like this year after year when I knew there was power in the Lord. It made me angry how the enemy had his way with him. Why can't you believe baby? My heart would break and I would be upset. It was a constant battle. Over the past couple of years, on several different occasions, I completed a 21-day Daniel fast. It didn't seem like anything significant happened at those times but I knew and could sense the Lord did something much greater than I could see. The unbelief, self-hatred that oppressed my husband was going to come down. And the reason why I knew this was because Derek wanted the Lord and I never stopped believing that. My husband was worth fighting for.

I do not understand what I do. For what I want to do I do not do, but what I hate I do. And if I do what I do not want to do, I agree that the law is good. As it is, it is no longer I myself who do it, but it is sin living in me. For I know that good itself does not dwell in me, that is, in my sinful nature. For I have the desire to do what is good, but I cannot carry it out. For I do not do the good I want to do, but the evil I do not want to do—this I keep on doing. Now if I do what I do not want to do, it is no longer I who do it, but it is sin living in me that does it. So I find this law at work: Although I want to do good, evil is right there with me. For in my inner being I delight in God's law; but I see another law at work in me, waging war against the law of my

mind and making me a prisoner of the law of sin at work within me.
What a wretched man I am! Who will rescue me from this body that
is subject to death? Thanks be to God, who delivers me through Jesus
Christ our Lord! (Romans 7:15-25)

Wherefore the law was our schoolmaster to bring us unto Christ,
that we might be justified by faith. But after that faith is come, we are
no longer under a schoolmaster. For ye are all the children of God by
faith in Christ Jesus. For as many of you as have been baptized into
Christ have put on Christ. (Galatians 3: 24-27)

The law is good because it shows us that we can't keep the law
in our own strength. We're prone to break it, it's meant to bring us
to the Lord Jesus Christ. It helps us to recognize that we can't obey
and walk in obedience without Him. We need His grace and mercy.
And when we abide in Him we will have the victory because of
Jesus Christ and His blood. We have put on Jesus Christ and He has
made us new in Him. The old man and its carnal nature and desires
dies so that the new man made alive by the Spirit of God within
begins to abound. It is no longer I that live but He that liveth in me
(Gal 2:20).

Although he wanted to, Derek didn't know how to hand things
over to the Lord. He would ask me how I did it. I would try to explain and it seemed simple to me. I handed things over to the Lord
by faith. But it didn't make sense to him how I did that. The Lord
kept reminding me to stay still and yield to Him. The Lord was
at work no matter how it looked right now. He was the one who
opened eyes to see and ears to hear. He knew my husband better
than I did. He was making a way for him even in the midst of my
frustration of waiting for his deliverance by sending me correction.

Are you always wondering what he's doing? There was a time in
the rough years of our marriage when I wondered what he was doing
at work, I wondered what was on his mind or who was on his mind.

And these kind of thoughts hurt me and got me angry inside to think that he could have another woman on his mind, maybe even while he was with me. These kinds of thoughts were tormenting and it was not a good place to be in. The Lord began to speak to me during this time because He does not want one of His children to endure life like that!! And we don't have to. He wants us to think on good things, pure thoughts (Philippians 4:8), because whatever we hold in our thoughts, will lead our actions. The Lord reminded me of a word one day that I had heard many times referencing a rebuke for those who want to judge another brother or sister in the Lord. But the Lord was speaking to me about it towards my husband. And yes although he is my husband, he was also my brother in the Lord. And the Lord was seeing something in me. I had a plank in my own eye.

> *And why beholdest thou the mote that is in thy brother's eye, but considerest not the beam that is in thine own eye? Or how wilt thou say to thy brother, Let me pull out the mote out of thine eye; and, behold, a beam is in thine own eye? Thou hypocrite, first cast out the beam out of thine own eye; and then shalt thou see clearly to cast out the mote out of thy brother's eye. (Matthew 7:3-5)*

There was something in my heart and I could sense Him leading me to the control and anger in my heart. Then to confirm and help me further along in understanding what He was speaking to me, I came across a book called, *The Peace Promise* by John Kuypers.[3] The first few pages spoke to me. As the Lord opened this to me, I understood that I had to come to an acceptance that in whatever way the Lord answered me, I had to let go of all expectations and let Him do as He pleases and accept the outcome. This brought me peace. The Lord showed me that anger and bitterness was the plank in my eyes. I was angry and bitter with my husband. Deep down I doubted that

Derek wanted freedom. I couldn't believe that his freedom would ever come. The anger and bitterness blinded me to what the Lord was doing and what He wanted to do in Derek's heart, and in my heart. I couldn't see anymore. I wanted to quit many times! It stole my joy and weighed me down. I didn't see Derek as the leader in our home anymore and I felt that I had to take control of our marriage. And this was only fueling my anger and bitterness even more. I wasn't being fruitful in this way.

As I read further, I understood that I had been expecting Derek to live up to my standard. What I needed to do was to release him to the Lord and let the Lord deal with him. It was going to have to be between him and the Lord. It would be then, free of any pressure from me, that he would have to be accountable for his actions and choices. By letting him go, I was free from taking control of the situation and was laying it all on the Lord and Derek.

We need to stay in a neutral position. When I am trusting the Lord for my marriage and my life, I can pray for my husband. I can love him. The Spirit can flow through my life and I can move and pray, believing in those prayers with a pure heart. And He will answer. It goes back to being in Christ and having His promises fulfilled for us. But it has to be all Him. He won't be moved to do anything out of our frustrations and anger. Stay neutral.

We continued with *My Nehemiah Wall*, and with each wall I prayed the Scriptures as I spent time with the Lord. I made videos and shared them online. There were so many marriages falling apart and we saw a few of them on our social media. I had known some that had given up on their faith and walked away from God. They got angry at Him and blamed Him for different things that happened to them in their lives or they were hurt from the church. They too were looking at themselves instead of looking to God and believed the lies of the enemy. They did not know the truth because they had not been discipled. And this is missing in our churches.

Whenever I would get discouraged Derek would tell me, stay on the wall. He was watching what I was doing online and he was seeing my love for the Lord and how I never quit. It was encouraging him to continue and to push onward. But I will be the first to say, it's all been the Lord!!

I have to drink from the Living Water. And I would not have learned how if not for all the battles I have come through already. The rejection from my dad and that side of my family hurt but it brought me closer to the Lord. The hurt I received from my marriage also brought me closer to the Lord. Every battle brought me to my knees. I would never want to go through any of those battles again, but I'm thankful for every part of it.

And did all drink the same spiritual drink: for they drank of that spiritual Rock that followed them: and that Rock was Christ. (1 Corinthians 10:4)

We have to drink from this Spiritual Rock who is Jesus. I was given His grace and strength. It's quite amazing. When I thought I would drown, He kept me. And when I went through the fire, I wasn't burned. The Lord is faithful. And so whatever you're going through, keep enduring. The Lord is going to answer you.

We had a few orders for the wall that come in and this kept us encouraged. I found my passion in the building of these walls. I saw the power of God behind His Word. Although beautiful, they were not just for decor, but their purpose was far greater than one could see. I was praying for my marriage, prodigals and family and friends. I was praying for my First Nations communities.

For the eyes of the Lord run to and fro throughout the whole earth, to show Himself strong on behalf of those whose heart is perfect toward Him. (2 Chronicles 16:9)

You may be in a season of praying for your loved ones or your spouse. Be encouraged that when the lies come from the pit of hell, or when distraction and discouragement comes, you have to persevere. Sanballet had did all that he could to try get Nehemiah off the wall. He wanted him to stop what he was doing so that the people would continue to be destroyed. His enemies came around taunting Nehemiah and told him that even the foxes could break down his wall. The enemy would say to you, 'Why pray, you're not doing anything and it's all a waste of time. And what can you do?'

We continued to push onward and the Lord kept pouring out His grace. His Word began flourishing and abounding in our hearts. Then came this one day. It was a Sunday morning service over at Summit. And when we got there, I could feel the spirit of lust stirring and I got upset. Derek would usually stop and pray with me whenever he could feel it. But he didn't at that time and I left him sitting there by himself and went outside. I decided to go for a walk outside or sit on a bench. I just needed to get away from him. It was a nice day and I loved the landscape at Summit. I sat down on the bench to enjoy this time alone, and I jumped on my Instagram and the first video I saw on my newsfeed was a wife talking about how to be Godly wives towards our husbands. She posted a couple of scriptures and I felt it hit me so hard. I felt the spirit of the Lord's conviction on me and it turned me right around and I marched back inside. It was a strong correction and I knew I needed to heed what He spoke to me. I joined my husband. He needed me and walking away from him wouldn't have been good.

The Lord was on the move. He was tearing things down and building up.

I was still walking the *100 Days Walking By Faith*. The group on Facebook was active and there were a few ladies still walking too. I battled with continuing at times because I felt the pressing on all sides. It was our finances, being in a smaller place, having to go to a laundromat, and having no money to do anything. And on top of all this I was dealing with parosmia for two years. Parosmia is a long COVID symptom. I couldn't eat meat, onions, spices especially garlic or eggs. They tasted rancid and rotten. My sense of smell and hearing wasn't right either. I know, it's been unreal and unbelievable. It's been two years since I've had this but what's even more weird is that I can eat all the sugar laden foods that I did before. I can have all the pastries and junk food I want! Now this would have been a treat for me in the past but I know it will cost me my health. I was prediabetic before and all this food was my downfall. And now I have to exert some discipline and lean on the Lord. It's like the giant of obesity rising up against me, and I have to war against it. It has not been fun. But I'm learning to let things go to the Lord, He pours out His grace and I'm strengthened again. He will deliver me from gluttony. He is using this to draw me closer to Him.

I don't cook as much for my family as I used to because of the smell. There is something psychological when that happens because if it doesn't smell good then, in my mind, the food must be bad. And it feels like I'm giving my family bad meat. As a result, Derek has had to cook more. It is bizarre how this has happened. But I know I will taste food again and I am now looking forward to the marriage supper.

Be encouraged whatever you're facing right now, it is meant to draw you closer to Him as well. You will not be consumed. The one who keeps you neither sleeps nor slumbers.

Indeed, he who watches over Israel never slumbers or sleeps.
(Psalm 121:4)

I was thankful to the Lord for my friend Doreen who had come to see me at the park in Yorkton. When I couldn't do it she helped me with the *100 Days Walking By Faith* group. The Lord had her keep her hand on it when I couldn't. And she continues to help me with it to this day.

My husband and I were being tried and tested in ways I never saw coming. But it is because His return is imminent and yet there are many who are still not preparing for Him. I had a dream one night that I saw myself sleeping in the bed and was suddenly snatched and taken to be with the Lord.

The mission had devotions every morning and it is mandatory that guests go to them. Derek would do them from time to time. And each time he did the devotions, men gave their lives to the Lord. Derek always had an anointing on His life and I could see why the enemy had tried hard to snuff his life and to steal his vision for his life. If the enemy can steal the vision or future from someone, he will. He is relentless and merciless and his only plans are to steal, kill and destroy anyone (John 10:10). The men that gave their lives to the Lord would come to Derek afterwards and tell him that he really spoke to their heart.

But Derek continued to have a hard time staying there. He was getting angry and frustrated from day to day. At times I felt really bad for him, and other times, I would smile knowing that he was exactly where the Lord wanted him to be and that He was going to strip him layer upon layer. I knew how Derek was feeling and it reminded me of when I went to look after my grandmother years before, back in Saskatchewan, when she was sick. She was out of the hospital and was home recovering. I was busy helping her with doing the cleaning and running her errands. But it wasn't long before she was scolding me as I was wiping and putting the dishes away. I remember getting angry and saying to myself, "I don't need this," and wanted to leave. But the Lord spoke to me, and said if I cannot serve her, that He couldn't take me any further than here. He wanted a heart that was ready to serve, and that included times of being uncomfortable. This included times of me obeying Him no matter how much I didn't want to do it. This meant carrying my cross and laying my desires down. I was laying down my selfishness, arrogance and my pride. I knew He knew what was good for me although I couldn't see it. I was choosing to obey and I was going to serve her as He wanted me to. I was not going to go back to who I used to be. That much was made up in my mind.

Derek knew the word of God more than anyone else I knew. I recall one of his first emails when we were first getting to know each other. He was responding to an email I sent him and I will always remember it. He replied, "How could I tell the potter how to shape me if I was the clay in His hand?" He was referring to the prophet Jeremiah. The Lord had told the prophet to go down to the potter's house and when he got there he saw the potter break down the clay he had in his hand and watched him sculpt a masterpiece. And the Lord asked him, O house of Israel, can I not do with you as this potter does?" declares the LORD. "Like clay in the hand of the potter, so are you in my hand." (Jeremiah 18:6)Time and time again, it has been this same passage of scripture that the Lord has used to speak to both of our lives.

I remember when I read his email at that time that it spoke to my heart. It showed me that he had a sincere heart to follow the Lord. We were all this marred piece of clay that needed to be molded, broken and shaped by His loving hands.

We have been all over Canada and now we're in the United States away from home. These were different times and the "normal" life we once knew was over. He was doing a new thing. The vision of darkness coming across Canada that my husband saw and the mandates brought us here. We knew we had to leave Canada for a while. Will He call us to return? I'm sure He will.

In the earlier years of our marriage, the Lord showed me my husband crying and broken, but He assured me that He would come for him. He also showed me that I would be with him on the journey. The Lord would move my heart to pray and intercede for my husband because He was going to do a deep work in him. Derek has said through the years that he saw me as this big bird and he was this little bird that couldn't keep up with me. I laughed at him but what I saw in that, that my calling was to stand and pray for him, and that the Lord gave him a wife to pray for him. He needed a praying wife because of the calling of God that he had on his life. So if he thought I was a big bird, he was yet to see what God was going to do through him and his life.

I stopped getting angry as much and stopped saying things to my husband. When I knew he was struggling or felt lust trying to rear its face, I stayed quiet. I had to get out of the way and trust Him. I wasn't going to hinder the moving of the Lord. The Lord didn't share His glory with anyone. And deliverance would be on His time and in His way. And in the waiting, I was called to praise and honor my husband and Him. I would not be moved by my feelings anymore or listen to the lies of the accuser any longer. Everything changed for me that day on the gravel road.

This is a walk by faith and when we wield our sword by holding up His Word, His Spirit is able to move freely into any situation. We are to be fully surrendered and dependent on Him. He wants to have full reign over our lives, our family and homes. He has to root out and pull down to change our circumstances (Jer 1:10).

My husband and I were one and He was continuing to make us one. I knew He was working deep in my heart as well. I was reminded of that time when we took a walk through the park in Prince George the first year of our marriage. When the Lord asked me if I would still love Him if he never offered me anymore then himself. At that time my answer was yes, but today my answer would be an astounding 1,000,000% yes. Through the hard years and the never-ending trials that we have come through, the Lord has met me in so many ways. He has been faithful to every part of my life. When I wanted to quit, he gave me the grace to keep going. When I wanted to hate, he gave me His love. When I thought I would fall, He helped me up. When I wanted to fight in my carnal ways, He showed me His mercy. He has carried me through it all, and after seeing Him, and all these moments that I've had with Him, what I have found and feel inside of me is a substance that seems so tangible and real; a substance of faith that I could not have gotten without all these battles. Now I know that even though I may have nothing I have everything and my joy is and my cup is overflowing. Who I am in the Lord is what will keep me. The things around us are passing. What I have within is worth much more than gold.

I loved working at the women's shelter. It was His hand to put me here among other women who needed help. I saw who I used to be many years ago. I'd been in many shelters. I can remember how every day seemed so long when I lived there as a single mother. And it was hard to be at the mercy of others and having to do what they tell you. Those ladies struggle on a daily basis and I thank the Lord that I have the chance to pray for them. The Lord will do the rest. I knew that our time here was for a season. It was all preparation for something ahead. I am here. I will pray for the ones I work with and the ones that come through. The extra income helped with our bills. I found it even more amazing that my mother worked at Bethesda too. She worked as a counselor on the second floor and I worked on the first floor as a house supervisor. This was a God thing. He had orchestrated all of it and there was no denying it.

We may have been working there but we were lame in our own lives and we needed to go to the Bethesda waters. We had to drink from the Rock. A diamond is mined and it has to go through extreme pressure and temperatures to see its value. We were feeling the pressure.

My husband was saved but there were things being uprooted and pulled down. And the Lord was going to bring incredible healing. He had not been discipled and now was that time.

Derek went down a path of watching porn years before we got married. He continued down that path for a long time. Although Derek grew up in a Christian home, the kids around him did not come from Christian families. Their homes were filled with alcohol, violence, and a lot of activity that children should not have been exposed to. And so he heard a lot of things that shaped his thoughts about alcohol and sex. When he talks about that time he said he was taught that it was a "man" thing to do to drink and get a girl. It was how many women you "could get" and you weren't a man unless you were getting "some" and it was the perception of his world. Pornography was just something that everyone viewed in either magazines or videos. To him, this was what "sex" was. He didn't know what intimacy really was. What Derek had seen and learned was not the way the Lord intended for sexual intimacy to be between two people. Sexual intimacy was a beautiful thing and Derek had never seen it like that before. And there are many in the ministry and those who sit in the church who are bound to pornography and all kinds of things that do not fulfill them. They run to broken cisterns that the Bible says will not give them life. Cisterns are pools or wells carved out from a rock. These broken cisterns cannot hold water. None of those things ever fulfilled Derek. It was a temporary thrill but there was no life.

For my people have committed two evils; they have forsaken me the fountain of living waters, and hewed them out cisterns, broken cisterns, that can hold no water.(Jeremiah 2:13)

People run to these cisterns, seeking refuge in places that offer them no life. I used to run to relationships that I knew were not good for me. I ran to alcohol and drugs that I thought would give me a good time. But I was empty. Nothing brought me joy. Until I gave my life to Jesus Christ.

The Lord is relentless in His pursuit of you. He will continue to call you. He gave up His life on the cross and died willingly to save you. The world likes to dispute this, calling it a lie and, without any fear or reverence, they curse His name. But did you ever stop and wonder why it is His name that's the most hated and cursed above every other name? He points people to their sin because He sees the train wreck ahead. He knows that sin will destroy lives. It strangles and suffocates its victim while leaving them in torment. Jesus was hated and those who killed Him wanted to shut Him down and silence His voice. But since the cross until now the Spirit of God is still moving.

I think of Stephen who was taken outside the city to be stoned to death. The Spirit of God had come to him after the resurrection of Jesus Christ. He and the apostles had all been filled with the Holy Ghost in an upper room. After they were filled they began to speak in other tongues and they went out and preached the gospel. Stephen was one of them who went out and he became the first martyr of Christendom. He told the religious leaders of his day all that the Lord had done since the time of Moses. And that enraged them and they took him and stoned him. Yet he loved them!!! They were blinded by their hate and religion. They were proud men. And I am in awe of what Stephen does next; he cries out to the Lord to forgive them and says do not hold this sin against them. His heart was burning with love for them all so they would come to salvation. Stephen was touched by the Lord and had been changed.

And this is what happens to those who experience meeting Jesus Christ. We're changed and there is no denying His presence.

And that he died for all, that they which live should not henceforth live unto themselves, but unto him which died for them, and rose again. (2 Corinthians 5:15)

The life we now live is for the Son who gave His life for us. This life is not ours. We would have destroyed each other if it was not for His love.

If you're hurting, keep looking to the Lord because He is in your midst right now working it out for you. You might not feel like it, or see it, but endure a little while longer and you will see it all come together.

Every time I hurt, every time I was pressed on all sides, it brought me down to my knees in prayer. I cried out and the Lord poured out His love on me. I loved my husband more deeply.

Father's Day

It was a season of stretching and we were having it hard financially. We had no extra money and it was Father's Day. But something amazing happened on that day. I decided to make the best of it and I was going to take him down to the lake. I took my Bible and my Bluetooth speaker, and a blanket. It was always beautiful down there. There is a walking and biking trail which runs along the river. After we parked, we found a nice place to sit by the riverbank. It was a special place for us because when we were homeless we stayed in a motel room that was up the street. We walked along the river every day. It's where we lived when my husband almost died of COVID.

We laid out our blanket and set up our speaker. We had a few minutes of complete contentment. At that moment it was just us in the world. And then, I opened my Bible and read the Word to him. And it was the most romantic thing I could have done for us. There we were without a dollar to our name but we had everything in our lives that mattered to us. It was His Word that kept us through the years and His Word that we have been building our marriage on.

We both had failed in the past and made some mistakes but by His mercy and grace He was giving us another chance to build our lives again His way.

We came across a training course by Francis Frangipane. It was called *In Christ's Image*. We decided on taking the course together. And as we worked through it, I could see the Lord bringing forth His healing in my husband. He had moments when the Holy Spirit touched something deep inside his heart. The Great Physician was at work and the timing of it was incredible. We needed this study. Derek harbored a lot of anger towards his mother and some of his family members for the way they treated me. They could not accept me and he said if they couldn't accept me then they couldn't have him either. He said they were the ones missing out. The word began to go deeper in his heart. It ministered to both of our hearts, and it spoke to me to get moving and finish my book. I had been working on this book although for the longest time I didn't know why I was writing it. We both experienced the pain of what happens when people who come to Christ are not discipled. They are moved into legalism and religion. The fruit of that is evident in hard and mean-spirited people. As we moved along in the course, it began confirming and affirming many things the Lord did in my life over the years. I never doubted what the Lord did in my life but it was a reminder that His calling in my life was still in motion.

It was clear that we were entering into a new season. And things were going to change for the better and freedom was coming. The Lord had everything in place and it was the appointed time for deliverance. *Behold, I will do a new thing; now shall it spring forth; shall ye not know it? I will even make a way in the wilderness, and rivers in the desert (Isaiah 43:19).*

We were reminded of the verse we had in our living room when we went through this course. It was this same verse I put up back in Canada before leaving to come to the United States. I could see how the Lord was moving and stirring my husband's heart as we went through the training.

I started thinking of the time when we lived back in Moose Factory. One afternoon, I watched my husband carving out a walking stick in the back yard. And I saw him being like a type of Moses and that one day He would call him out and separate him unto Himself. He would have to be moved far away from what was comfortable to him. But I really felt then that the calling in my husband was great.

And now, here we were on new soil and in a new country. And in time the Lord would prepare my husband to preach the gospel.

Derek continued to yield his life to the Lord. But there were still times that the spirit of lust would rear its ugly head and I hated it. But when would he hate it?

The Lord spoke to my heart how these temptations that would come would be a tool He used in His hands to draw my husband to Himself. And these temptations would come and show the weight of sin that could not be overcome by his own doing. He was powerless over it and his only hope was in the Lord.

In the next building over beside ours an attractive young girl moved in. She was never a subject until I began to see her lit up lights at night. Her living room would light up blue or red in her living room. Her drapes would be wide open. It wasn't a smart thing to do because she lived on the ground floor. But it wasn't long before she caught the attention of my husband's eyes.

The Lord would use this and I knew it was a trying of Derek's heart. The Lord knew she was there and I knew but I wasn't going to let it bother me. At times it still did and hurt but I continued to run to the Father. But He would use it for His glory and for our good.

What do we do when no one is watching us? Do we visit questionable websites when no one is around? Do we go to places where we know we will be tempted? Temptation will always be around us but we don't have to yield to it. The truth is that whatever we love and enjoy doing we will make time for. If we love the Lord we will put everything else down for Him. And I had to put my husband in the Lord's hands.

With her enticing speech she caused him to yield, With her flattering lips she seduced him. Immediately he went after her, as an ox goes to the slaughter, Or as a fool to the correction of the stocks, Till an arrow struck his liver. As a bird hastens to the snare, He did not know it would cost his life. (Proverbs 7:20-23)

The word describes the power behind the spirit of lust. And there are many men who are seduced by following this spirit. They will be compelled to her door and enter into her destruction. And it will cost him everything. And there are women waiting for nothing more than to seduce men, especially godly men.

We decided to park further away from her apartment rather than park in front of her balcony. It was our way of doing due diligence to guard ourselves and to protect our marriage. We make sure that we are not alone with the opposite sex. We don't leave room for the enemy to give anyone something to talk about. And we don't have friends of the opposite sex.

Gideon

The Israelites had done evil in the sight of God and because of their disobedience God had given them over to their enemies, the Midianites. For seven years the Israelites had been under heavy oppression. And at harvest time, the Midianites would come into their camps and take all their food.

Then one day, an angel appeared before Gideon. He called Gideon, a mighty man of valor. It's believed that this angel was actually the Lord Jesus in His incarnate form, or His form before being born into the world. He told Gideon to go and he would destroy the Midianites. But Gideon struggled with that saying that he was the least in his family. He was feeling like a nobody but he was definitely not a mighty man of valor. He asked for a fleece, or a sign, and the Lord gave it to him. And when he battled his enemies, the Lord sent him with only 300 men. And it was purposed like that so Gideon would know that it was God who delivered him, and not the work of his army. It had nothing to do with the strength of Gideon or his army, but it had everything to do with God, delivering him. And this is where we must all come to, and believe that it has to be all Him to overcome all our enemies.

Derek battled with the thought that the Lord had called him to do anything because of how he felt about himself. And this may be your struggle right now. What are you believing? Do you believe that your life has no purpose? This is not true, for the Lord is looking for someone to inhabit, and who will trust Him.

5:15 Mornings

Derek began a Bible study called, "The Testing of Your Faith", by Bruce Wilkinson. It was in this study that Derek saw his name in a Bible passage. His name "Derek" in Hebrew meant "way".

> *Jesus saith unto him, I am the way, the truth, and the life: no man cometh unto the Father, but by me. (John 14:6)*

Pointing Derek to Jesus could not have been clearer. It made sense to me when we first started talking when I said that there was something different about his name. He was blown away and I was further blown away.

Then he told me that he wanted to wake up at 5:15 in the morning to pray and get into the word. He wanted to get closer to the Lord because he was really tired of where he was. He was tired of living in unbelief and wanted more of the Lord. But I must admit when I heard him say that, I didn't think he would stick to it. I knew him well and we have gone down this road several times before. He would start something and do it for a few days or a few weeks if it was going well and then he would quit. I knew he had it in his heart to do something for the Lord, but he had it all wrong in the sense that he figured he had to do good works for the Lord to love him. He couldn't comprehend Jesus' love for him already.

But every morning he got up at 5:15 to seek the Lord and to pray. When I asked how it was going, he would tell me it was hard but he dragged his feet and went. He got up every morning like clockwork and it didn't matter how tired he was. I knew the first few days were rough for him. It was hard for a long time because he didn't have any breakthroughs and I knew it was disappointing to him. But he kept going. I told him one day how the Lord waited for him every morning and knew when he was coming down the hallway. This really encouraged him but I knew the Lord was waiting for my husband to come have fellowship with Him. It's been several months now of him waking up at 5:15 and things are completely different now in His walk with the Lord.

There were many mornings that he would come back to the bedroom singing. Something was happening. Something was changing. The religious works and deadness that would cover my husband at times seemed to be dying. Then he wanted to do a seven-day water fast. And I can remember thinking that he couldn't do water fast, he's diabetic and every time he's tried in the past, his sugars got too low. It wasn't good for him. But if the Lord called him to do it, he would be able to do it. I can remember the opposition that came for him from all sides. It was funny when he messaged from work and told me his coworkers and the guests were coming to him with food. And asking if he wanted anything! There was everything coming in to tempt him from cupcakes to pizza! But he kept going and said no to everything, he never gave in to those cupcakes. And up until that point, the offer of food did not happen to him. We knew undoubtedly that it was the Lord who had called him to this fast. The incredible part about this fast was that his sugar levels didn't drop. His sugar remained good and that was incredible. I was amazed by watching all of it.

We knew this was from the Lord and He was sustaining him in this fast. After he was done his seventh day, he was in the room. I had come in and he was laid out on the floor. And when he got up he told me that he knew that the lies that the enemy had been speaking to him for years were not actually a part of him. For years, he had believed these lies. He believed that these lies defined who he was. But he suddenly realized they were from without, and not from within. He knew these lies were no longer true and had no hold over his life. This was a breakthrough that I didn't see coming, and then he prayed for his mother. The Lord spoke to him, that he could not hold onto his sense of being justified and harboring anything against her, but he had to forgive her, like Jesus forgave him. We got into prayer and he forgave her that night of everything and he felt love again in his heart for her. There were more tears for the Lord to store.

The New Covenant

The following weeks would be miracle after miracle in my husband's life. It had been a couple of years before all these things started happening when I had heard a sermon from Carter Conlon. It was on the New Covenant and I recognized John 17 when he started talking about it. I can remember crying and praying out that chapter in my bedroom for my husband. I didn't realize the power, and the promise, behind that word until then. It amazed me. I don't even think I started writing for this book consistently at this point. But seeing how the Lord would come again and again with this word, it was more evident that I needed to write. The Lord wants the world to know that we don't get to heaven on our good works. It is by faith and believing in the Son of God who died on the cross for our sins. He redeemed us for Himself and restored that relationship that was once broken. He brought us out of darkness into the light. And when we abide and rest in Him, we will triumph through Him.

One morning Derek went to work and his coworker told him to look at John 17 and to study it. And see what he saw through reading it. He was surprised by this because he knew it was the chapter I had on my prayer wall during the time he had left us.

This was an "only God could do this" stunned moment. I couldn't believe what the Lord was doing. He was leading my husband directly to the scriptures that I had on my wall. I told my husband that I didn't know why I put John 17 on my wall, but I had seen a dialogue between Jesus and the Father. The Father had granted to Jesus that everyone who received Jesus as their Lord and Savior, the Father would keep them for Him because they belonged to Him. I knew that Derek had accepted Jesus as Lord and Savior, and that the Lord would keep Derek because He had the power to do it.

Then the same chapter would come again but this time to my husband. He had listened to a sermon by David Wilkerson. I remember when he first told me about it, I could see the joy all over his face as he received the revelation that we are in the world, but we are NOT of it. It was a moment between him and the Lord. He was here, but his spirit was united with God in heaven.

John 17 is a chapter to read and study because it is a covenant promise for all those who believe in Jesus. We can walk in all the promises that the Lord has given us. The Lord promises to keep us so we would be with Him. We become one with Him like the Father and His Son are one. He promises to keep all that turn their hearts to His Son. It doesn't matter what we have done when we ask for forgiveness, He forgives us. His blood covers us.

An Act of Surrender

Derek was at work one day and he was witnessing to one of the guests. He asked Derek, "How do you surrender?" Another one of his coworkers came by and started witnessing to the guest too. His co-worker said, "You have to surrender and give everything up!" And to further illustrate his point, he got down on his knees and began crying out "Jesus, you have to help me! I can't do this on my own!" He showed them what it looks like when someone who is broken and needs help, or in need of deliverance, begins to honestly cry out to Jesus in desperation. "I need you Lord! Forgive me for sinning against you! I need you Jesus!" You need to make that cry and surrender every day. Neither the man that he was ministering to nor my husband had anything to say, but it deeply touched their hearts. They all needed to have that visual presentation of what it means to surrender to the Lord.

There are some people who, at one time, believed in God and they have drifted away. They've stopped believing in God, or believed they could live this life, and they've believed that they can live without God and do well on their own. Regardless of your status, the weight of sin can take the life out of anyone. Mental health problems are soaring in society and many people don't know where to go or where to turn.

When Derek left for another city to start his life over, he believed in a lie that he could do what he wanted. And that was a lie that has come down through the generations from the Garden of Eden. We read about it in the book of Genesis where the deceiver came to tempt Eve. He deceived her into believing that she and Adam could be like God knowing good and evil. She heard this and saw that the fruit was good to the eye. And together, they ate. The lie is that we can be our own god and do as we want. We are deceived into believing that this is our life. The reality is that these lives belong to

God. And one day we will have to give account to God for the lives we have lived.

Our Anniversary

It was our anniversary and again we had no money to even go for supper. I must admit, I was feeling the lack of money this time round. But Derek said he was going to make some food and wanted to go to a park. I knew he was checking for some parks online and he found one. We packed up and left for our anniversary date. My hubby is romantic and that day he was more attentive to me. He opened my car door, something he always does, and we walked a block and a half to the park. The park was named the Five Senses Gardens. It was unique and I'd never seen anything like it. The park was divided into five sections for the five senses: sight, hearing, taste, touch and smell. We didn't taste anything there but our other four senses were arrested by what we saw around us. As we walked along the path going from one section to the next, the Lord began to speak to my heart about deception, how it appeals to us in many forms, to our flesh, and to all our senses. If it feels good, sounds good, then it must be good. And there are many who fall into that trap. The touch section with its beautiful flowers was alluring and beautiful and it brought many to them and they fall into bondage of sin. Like people who are given over to flashy toys and nice possessions, they stay bound and never come to the fullness of knowing Jesus. Their love for the Lord grows cold. There is a lot of deception which is why we need to stay near the Lord. And we must not fulfill the lusts of the flesh or the pride of life. (1 John 2:15,16; Eph 2:3)

Fifteen

You Shall Be Like A
Watered Garden

And he said unto me, My grace is sufficient for thee: for my strength is made perfect in weakness. Most gladly therefore will I rather glory in my infirmities, that the power of Christ may rest upon me. (2 Corinthians 12:9)

It's hard to talk about these deeper issues of the heart but they are real. I was not one to suppress things. I didn't like the feeling of carrying the weight of these heart issues around. It is far better to put them in the all-powerful hands of the Lord.

"What's the matter?" he asked. Derek sat down at the end of the bed because he knew something was up with me. He could read me well. He always knew when I was feeling upset or down. I was never good at hiding anything. I was missing him and our time alone together and things had been so busy lately. It had been a long time since we had any type of a date night. And we were soon leaving on a trip. I was excited to go but I needed my husband too.

I was missing the intimacy and I told him how I was feeling and how he seemed distant towards me. He said it was because of diabetes that he had no sexual desire but I told him "No, it's because lust is not in your thoughts anymore." He had nothing anymore to push his 'feel good buttons' so to speak. "And now," I said, "it's destroyed our marriage."

"So drawing closer to the Lord has destroyed our marriage?" he said. I responded and said, "No of course not, but our marriage needs healing."

And he went into prayer for it and this was a major turn in our marriage.

In the past whenever I would bring anything up that wounded me he would become angry and defensive. But he was letting me talk and he was listening!

Even though I knew what I was sharing would have made him feel dumped on, he didn't make excuses or get angry. His prayer was genuine and right from his heart. He heard me and we both knew and he was partially right, because diabetes does play a role in sexual dysfunction, but it was also because lust was losing its power over him and intimacy became harder because he wasn't feeding off those "feeling good" pushes anymore. And it was hard to accept that lust, (these superficial images) had to be a thing in his mind to peak his arousal. That's what porn does to the mind. It uses fantasies to fulfill the mind and it gets used to that. It's a dopamine hit for the body and I can't compete with those superficial images on a screen. It felt like he had no sexual desire for me at times. And it cut deeply. I know he has a desire for me and I don't question his love for me either. He has been open and honest since day one. I told Derek long ago to never use those images when you are intimate with me. He gave me his word and said he wouldn't do that. But I knew what was happening throughout his day.

Where there is no vision, the people perish: But he that keepeth the law, happy is he. (Proverbs 29:18-19)

I knew the enemy had been blinding my husband's vision with these perverse images. If he didn't repent and yield to the Lord I knew they would ultimately destroy him. I couldn't leave him there in that place. I once believed that men were visual creatures, and that they could only be sexually stimulated visually. Now I understand that this is not entirely true. When we choose to believe this we inexcusably remove the responsibility and accountability from men who should be taking ownership over their slavery to sexual sin.

Sin entered the hearts of men because of a choice. Adam chose to disobey God, not just because he saw something. It was a choice he made that allowed sin to enter the heart of the entire human race. When the choice to sin was made, Satan gained mastery over every human being from Adam on, except for one. One who chose to obey God in every imaginable way. In thought, deed, and action, Jesus Christ fulfilled the will of the Heavenly Father. His love for the Heavenly Father kept Him in sinless perfection right to the cross. Without a love and desire for the Father's pleasure and will, men will always fail and fall into sin's snare. In order to walk as Jesus walked, we need the help of the Holy Spirit. Jesus called Him our Helper.

When we walk in the Spirit and walk closely to the Lord, we will be moved by how He moves. His Word tells us to walk as He walked. When we do this we can commune with the Lord every minute of the day without hindrance. He will always be in our thoughts and be with us. And as Christ sees, so will we see. Even as He sees women, we will see them with the same righteous eyes as His. But men have made women a sexual object to fulfill their sexual lust and selfish pleasures. And this should not be so, especially within the church body. This is something that breaks and grieves the heart of God.

The plan of the enemy is to destroy the lives and blind the vision of our men and husbands so that they cannot see what the Lord desires to do for them. His plan is to topple men from their divinely appointed position of being the spiritual leaders of their home and communities. Instead our men are humiliated by hell's demonic forces and are blinded by their own lust. We need to cover our men – both young and old – in prayer because they are in spiritual battles that we cannot see without the Lord's help. There are so many trapped in the snare of pornography.

The world sees pornography as normal and that it's a "man" thing to do (*although there are women ensnared as well*). But it's not a godly thing to do. The enemy has perverted the marital bed and has made it cheap.

The marital bed is beautiful and it's about giving and serving one another. As my husband presses into the Lord and humbles himself to pray, there is a real love and fulfillment coming into our marriage. It's rich and beautiful. I have let go of all the hurt. The more that I embrace God's love and press into His love, it washes everything away. It's lost its hold on me to hurt me anymore. That's because I have chosen to look to the Lord and I know that in time He perfects all of us. We're all needing change and the Lord will use whatever he chooses to bring to death everything not of Him in our lives.

I began to notice how tender and loving my husband was becoming. He was changing the more he kept waking up to meet with the Lord in the morning. It has been surreal.

I remember one morning as Derek and I were driving to his work. On the days I had to work, I went with him and dropped him off. We share one vehicle. On the way to work one morning, he shared with me about a word the Lord had given him. As he was doing his Bible reading that morning, he came across a word in Psalm 119. It was the last verse of that chapter.

I have gone astray like a lost sheep; seek thy servant; for I do not forget thy commandments. (Psalm 119:176)

"Lord, I know your word, but I need you to come for me," and that was his cry to the Lord that morning. "Lord, I know your word but you have to come for me!" He didn't know how to get to Him but was asking Him to come for him. I could see the hardness all beginning to come down. He wasn't faking anything, but was sincere. He didn't know how to find the Lord but he was crying out for the Lord to come to him. And this was all the Lord's doing. He was drawing him to Himself.

And this is what the Lord has been doing. He has been faithfully coming to meet him.

Then one evening a few days later as he was taking Nikki out, he said that as he got down to the end of the parking lot, he could feel darkness all around him. He felt fear like he never had before.

And it was the following morning that he was reading in the book of Job that he saw these scriptures.

God has made me sick at heart; the Almighty has terrified me. Darkness is all around me; thick, impenetrable darkness is everywhere. (Job 23:16-17)

The Lord was opening his eyes to the spiritual things around him. We were no match against the enemy on our own. The enemy will clean the streets with you. We need Jesus, our Savior, to walk every day. He is mighty and we are powerless over the enemy, but in Christ Jesus, we are more than conquerors. But without Him, we're powerless to do anything. It is foolish of us to think that we can live this life on our own when the truth is that we all desperately need the Lord. To live with such arrogance and pride is a scary place to be. We should walk before the Lord in humility and surrender.

A Banquet

This is where our story gets more amazing. I cannot believe it for myself, and I was there, but it's all true.

Our workplace hosts a yearly banquet, and as employees, we are expected to attend. While it's not mandatory, they strongly encourage all employees to go. And so, we signed ourselves up. It was a big event because all those who donated to the mission came and everybody was dressed up. As the day approached, I know both of us felt uneasy about it, because being in public was not something we looked forward to. On the day of the banquet we had a minor argument but we took it to prayer. I said that we needed to go and it was time for us. We were going to go and enjoy this time together. We didn't have to be subjected to the lies and voices of the enemy. I felt strengthened and excited. The Lord has given us power to tread over all the power of the enemy and nothing by any means shall hurt us (Luke 10:19).

When we got to the banquet, we noticed the tables had been elegantly set. And the color of the table napkins completely matched our wedding colors. It was like the table was set with us in mind. It was beautiful. We were seated with three men and Derek was at ease and talked with them. As the tables were served and we finished our dinner, we noticed the screen against the wall behind us. Derek told me to look and when I did, I saw the words, *"Behold, I Make All Things New."*

We both looked at each other and we just couldn't believe it. And if that wasn't enough, the Men's Mission Director got up to share. Because Derek knew him it made what happened next much more personal. As he spoke, he shared the following Bible verse,

*And the LORD shall guide thee continually, and satisfy thy soul
in drought, and make fat thy bones: and thou shalt be like a watered
garden, and like a spring of water, whose waters fail not. (Isaiah 58:11)*

This was my verse! This was my promise from years before when I first gave my life to Jesus Christ. An elderly lady, who was sitting behind me in a church service, had given me this same verse on a piece of paper. I had no clue what it meant. But now I understand. I was barren, meaning I was empty in my understanding of who Christ was, and who He was to me. I was ignorant in my understanding, until I began to open my heart to Him as I read the Scriptures. As I read and pressed into the things of the Lord more and more, He started to reveal to me who He was. I have experienced promise after promise knowing who the Lord is in my life. I saw how my life had become like a watered garden to those who had watched and seen God move upon my life. I have learned where to run to, I know how to answer anyone who asks me of the hope that is in me. I've learned to rest in Him. It is because of this that the river of living water flows through my life. I understand this now. We need to be yielded to Him. When we do this, His life will overflow out to others. We would've missed this moment had we listened to the lies of the enemy and stayed home from the banquet.

Some will see all of the goodness of God but will listen to the lies and the voices of others. They will miss the most beautiful and incredible gift that he is so lovingly preparing for us. He is preparing a banquet table for all of us when we come into His eternal kingdom.

He has given us His grace and mercy to endure all things. We will stand before Him without excuse.

* * *

An Oil Lamp

Our neighbors from downstairs moved out, and it was sudden. We left that afternoon and came back and they had everything moved out. I went knocking on their door to find out because if they found another place in the area, I wanted to move. But they were leaving the state. They asked us if I wanted their grill. It was brand new and they never used it. I quickly answered, "Yeah, sure." They helped me take that upstairs to my apartment. They had stuff sitting on their porch that they were throwing out and I noticed a glass lamp. And I went over and asked about it and they said take it. It was perfect, I had wanted to get a lamp like this for the longest time because it reminded me of the ten virgins. Five of the virgins were ready, and had their lamps full of oil, but the other five were foolish. They were not ready, and they missed the bridegroom when he came. The door was shut and they were cast out forever. I was going to make sure my lamp was full.

Something is Happening

One evening, before I left for work, I had a heavy burden on my heart for my family, my children, siblings, and my husband. I longed for them to come to the knowledge of who Jesus Christ is, to know His fullness, and that they would no longer be kicked around by the enemy. Derek came in to see me. I knew I was holding something in my heart against him. *'Why can't you believe?'* was the thought that ran through my mind. But it was then that the Lord reminded me that Derek was still getting up at 5:15 am every morning. And that was huge because Derek did not like getting up in the mornings. I asked him how he was doing? He responded that it was rough and I knew that he was discouraged again. He was in a place of self-loathing once again. Seeing this discouraged me. And as he left the room, I felt the heaviness. I had felt the conviction of the Lord to pray but instead of praying, I got on my phone. A few minutes later,

Derek came back into the room and I could see it written all over his face – the Lord had spoken to him.

Derek started exclaiming as he came into the room "Just thank Him!" Over and over again, he kept saying "Just thank Him!" He started thanking the Lord for his job, for bringing us here, for our home, and for our salvation. He was thanking the Lord for everything that He had done for us. Tears were streaming down his face as he praised the Lord for all that He had done. Then he came to lay down on the bed beside me and told me that he knew something had fallen off of him. "Something happened," he said. "I feel different. I feel like a new man. I feel like I can fly! It almost feels like the time I gave my life to the Lord. He did something. I don't know what He did, but I know I feel different!" I could sense that this was truly the Lord.

Derek had many more moments like this. The layers were being stripped away. This was a fulfillment of another one of the scriptures I had on my wall that I prayed over him. I had prayed that he would become a new man.

And the Spirit of the Lord will come upon thee, and thou shalt prophesy with them, and shalt be turned into another man. (1 Samuel 10:6)

When we pray and hold fast to His promises, He will answer, because He loves you. And like Hosea, who went out and brought Gomer back to himself, the Lord will do all that He can to bring you back to Himself, and to restore you back into right relationship with Him. He will relentlessly pursue you.

I came home from doing the laundry and Derek sat with me while I put our clothes away. He started talking to me about the word and God but I heard something else in Him this evening. There was a hunger for truth. My husband began talking and I could hear the joy and love in His voice for the Lord. He was talking like a new man. Someone else was coming forth. I heard a notification on my phone and checked it. I told him my videos were being shared and he asked me what was the most recent one. I checked and handed him the phone to listen to it. And I was reading from Psalm 103. I had no clue. I was folding clothes again and my mind was focused on putting them away. He said to me. "Are you serious?" I didn't know what he meant, but he said, "That's the word that saved me!"

The video had hit him. Derek said "This is the Psalm that saved me. It was this Psalm the Lord used to save me. I had been surrounded by darkness and this one day as I was reading this Psalm, a light broke through the darkness around me." This was a time when the spirit of suicide came heavy upon him and he cried out to the Lord to save him. He opened the Bible and as he read Psalm 103 the Lord pushed back the darkness around him for a moment. Later that night when that same darkness tried to swallow him, he could see a noose and how to tie it. He was so afraid because he felt that if help didn't come in some way, he was going to hang himself that night. In desperation he got on the phone and called a 1-800 prayer line. As the prayer counselor prayed, Derek could not believe what he was hearing! The prayer counselor was praying the words of Psalm 103. It was the same word he read from earlier that day. God spared him that day.

This caused Derek to cry. I knew it hit him and he said, "I need to pray." He started to pray in a way that I had never heard him pray before. Then after he was done praying, I went to sit beside him. With tears in his eyes, he looked at me and began to tell me how beautiful I was. He told me how God saw me a long time ago and He knew that I was gonna love Him. I could see the Spirit of the Lord upon him, and I knew the Lord was talking to him. I put my arms around him and we held each other and both cried. There was such a powerful presence of God in the room with us. I was holding my best friend, my husband. We knew that the Lord was in the midst of us. Derek said it was like He was standing right beside us. It was the most amazing incredible experience.

There is a day coming when everything you're going through is all going to make perfect sense. The Lord is going to reveal the answers to every question we have ever had. As eternity unfolds it will all be known to us.

Pray and draw near to the Lord. Whatever you're waiting on the Lord for, He will answer. Stay on your wall and continue to build your wall of prayer. The louder the lies become against us, we can trust that His truth is around the corner and we will see deliverance. We have been amazed by what the Lord has done.

Derek

My wife always told me that I reminded her of Moses. I never really understood what she meant. I was walking down the road with a walking stick that I had carved from a piece of tree branch and she later told me I reminded her of Moses. I felt like she was kind of making fun of me with my walking stick and didn't really want to pay attention to the comparison.

But it was only recently that I understood more of what she was talking about.

In the land of Egypt the people of Israel were slaves. They were under the hand of cruel and evil taskmasters. They were probably subjected to cruel taunts and horrible insults. Day after day they were reminded that their only worth was found in the work they did for the Egyptians. The work they did was monumental and worthy of praise from men. But what they accomplished was only done under a regime of cruel and heavy oppression and a form of religious duty. And yet, they continued to believe in and give what little worship they could to the God of their father Abraham. But under the heavy hand of their masters they continued as slaves for 400 years. Yet, even the Egyptians realized the strength and power that their slave labor force possessed if they were to rise up against their oppressors. And so, their strategy was to keep the Israelites in bondage to works and under the thumb of oppression.

Religion keeps people in bondage and is a very cruel taskmaster. I'm not talking about organized religion. I am talking about the spirit of religion, although most, if not all, organized religion is under the control of an evil principality of religion. Religion feeds and fuels man's pride. It blinds them to the bondage they are in. Religion deceives its captives into believing that they are doing worthwhile things while living in slavery. And it is always slavery to sin. It might be slavery to the good works, or to gossip, back-biting, or even perverse and sexual sins. In my case, it was slavery to good works, ministry, and sexual sin. And the voice of my oppressor would always make me feel worthless and ashamed while yet allowing me the satisfaction of doing "works."

Moses knew that he would one day be the deliverer for the Israelites. The Bible gives us evidence that Moses sensed the call to fight for his people and lead them out of slavery. But his attempts to do this were in his own strength. His attempts to deliver his people were futile and puny compared to what God had in mind. Moses, unlike the Israelites, was living in Egypt as a free man, but yet, he was bound to a religious taskmaster as well. His taskmaster pushed him to lean on his works over God. Moses' works were found in his education, his prominent standing in Pharaoh's court, and in the belief that he was destined to be a leader. All of this fueled his passion and lust for power and recognition. He wanted to be "the man." And this was also in my heart.

Religion is insidious. It makes you believe that all you are doing is so good, so worthwhile, and so noble, but behind the shiny exterior lies a dark and evil slave master who wants you to walk in your own pride and arrogance instead of surrendering to the Lord for complete deliverance. The voice of religion is clever but it can be discerned. "You can do it in your strength. Yes, you can cry out to God, but He wants you to fight for yourself. Keep doing what you are doing. It's good and it makes you feel good."

Coming to the Cross of Christ requires surrender, obedience and humility. It means giving up your life to all that God wants to do. It means living your life for the sake of God and others rather than for yourself. Jesus did not seek after titles. He called Himself the Son of man, never once did He refer to Himself as the Son of God. He associated with those He came to serve. He came to give His life as a ransom. He came in a completely surrendered posture before His heavenly Father to the point where he suffered a cruel criminal's death for our salvation. For us, this kind of surrender lacks the prestige or recognition we desperately hunger for among men.

The Pharisees loved the attention and praise of men. They lusted and thirsted for the accolades and praise of their peers and those they deemed to be beneath them. In their eyes Jesus was the antithesis of everything they had built and believed in. He was a rebel to their religion. And they wanted nothing to do with Him because he brought nothing to honor or serve them. This is the spirit of religion. It wants you to serve it. It wants you to bow down to it. It wants you to follow it. It wants you to live under its rule and oppression. Its deceitful reward is prominence and pleasures. At its core is lust. Remember how the Israelites longed for the pleasures of Egypt when they were in the desert?

> And the mixt multitude that was among them _fell a lusting_: and the children of Israel also wept again, and said, Who shall give us flesh to eat? We remember the fish, _which we did eat in Egypt freely_; the cucumbers, and the melons, and the leeks, and the onions, and the garlick: But now our soul is dried away: there is nothing at all, beside this manna, before our eyes. (Numbers 11:4-6)

They easily forgot the cruelty and evil oppression they faced, but loved the rewards of their labors there. Lust was the root cause of their desires. They wanted the pleasures of Egypt because of lust. They were slaves in Egypt but yet, in their minds they believed that they were free in Egypt! This is what religion does. It causes you to be bound and led by your lusts, while living under oppression, believing in an illusion of freedom.

This has been Satan's grand deception and lie from day one to Adam and Eve in the Garden of Eden. "Surely God would not withhold pleasures from you? He created you to enjoy all things. In fact, you should be able to decide for yourself what is good and right for you! It's okay to sin because you won't die from it. Instead YOU will be like God and be free like He is to decide what is right for YOU. You really are only doing a good thing by doing this for yourself." It is deceptive and selfish. And once you fall prey to this deceptive lie, lust becomes the primary evidence of the presence of this religious spirit.

When the eyes of Adam and Eve were opened, they saw that they were naked and covered themselves. Suddenly, once their eyes had been opened, a shame fell upon them like a cruel taskmaster. But it was too late, lust was now conceived and had brought sin, shame, and death. And lust had been conceived under the parentage of religious works of doing something good to satisfy self. Lust will kill your life, your home, your marriage and your future. Adam and Eve were never the same again and their relationship with God was completely destroyed. Wherever a religious spirit has power, lust will always be present in one form or another.

God had a plan for Moses' life. He would be the man God would send to Pharaoh to finally free the Israelites from 400 years of oppression and slavery. But it would take a complete separation from Egypt. It needed Moses to be taken out of Egypt and into the wilderness to be delivered from Egypt. And like Moses, I had to be taken out of the environment that religion and lust ruled over. Yes, I said it, I had to be taken out of the organized church religion to be delivered from religion and lust.

Many young anointed ministers of the gospel have sincere desires to be instruments in the hands of God, but because the spirits of religion and lust abound in the atmosphere of organized church, they become targets of these demonic spirits. They become enamored by the prestige that comes with singing or preaching before the crowds. The travel, recognition, and honorariums become their focus. It becomes a fuel for lust. And religion covers it all up nicely with a pretty bow of good works and satisfaction. Please don't misunderstand me; there are many sincere Christians seeking to do the Lord's will, carrying their cross in humility and surrender. However, for every one of them, there are many more bound by religious works and lust.

I was trapped in religious works and lust. And the Lord has brought me into the wilderness to see who I was and to set me free from the stranglehold that held me bound and oppressed. I am seeing now after several years just how deeply held in bondage I was. My heart cries for those young people who are falling into the same place of bondage I was in. Today, like Moses, I am coming to face this Pharaoh and to say, "Let my people go!" I want my First Nation peoples to walk in freedom. The Lord desires for each and every one of His people to walk as free and to be free from the bondages of religion and lust. He is doing that for me today. And I know He will do it for you as well.

I was speaking with one of the men from the Men's Mission. We had gone out on a food outreach to a small community and after we had handed out the food we gathered together for pizza. We sat down at the table and started talking. I told him that we were in the final process of editing this book and he asked what it was about. I began explaining to him that this book was about the struggle of marriage and how lust hurts a marriage, dealing with wounds and hurts in a marriage, and how we are changed by God in the marriage. He exclaimed, "Wow that's something everyone deals with. And to teach people how to resist lust is good." I immediately responded, without thinking, that it is not about resisting sin, it's about letting Christ live in us and finding victory when we give him our lives.

When the evening ended, I texted my wife to let her know we were done and she came to pick me up. We talked about our day briefly and I mentioned the discussion I'd had with the gentleman from the mission. I asked her if we could get some gas, a drink, and go for a drive together. I wanted to spend some time with her. She liked the idea so off we went. After fueling up we pulled up to McDonalds and ordered a drink. As we pulled up to the window, lust rose up within me as the girl took our payment. It shook my whole inner being and my wife asked me, "Are you OK?" I replied, "No, I feel it all over me and it's causing me to shake inside. I hate this! It's disgusting and ugly. I want it gone!" I'm not hiding this anymore. I'm not giving it a dark place to grow. I'm bringing it into the light and it will be in the light of Christ that I will find freedom.

As we pulled away, I knew my wife was affected by it as well. She told me that she could feel it too. I thank God that the Lord has given my wife discernment. I remember early on when lust would rise up within me, I didn't hate it like I do now. I allowed it to rule over me. I gave it room to play and grow. As time went on I started to get worse and soon saw how truly evil and enslaved I was. I was a slave to the sin. I didn't realize that she could discern when this spirit was active. When I understood what it did to her I tried hard to resist this enemy whenever it would rise up, but it would only become stronger and stronger. I had to learn that victory over this enemy does not come through resistance, but through surrender and repentance. Resisting lust sounds noble. But it's actually prideful. Resisting lust relies on human will and strength.

Submit yourselves therefore to God. Resist the devil, and he will flee from you. (James 4:7)

Do you see what we are to do before even resisting? Submission to God! The Oxford Dictionary defines submission *as the action or fact of accepting or yielding to a superior force or to the will or authority of another person.* Before we can even find ANY strength in resisting the devil, we have to come to a place of submission to God. Submission can only be achieved when we believe that there is a superior power than our own. We have to believe that God is able to deliver. We have to believe that He will set us free. We have to believe that He is able to do above all that we ask or think. This has been my battlefield – unbelief! I could not believe that I would ever be free. I believed God could and would set others free, but for whatever reason, I couldn't believe for myself. I was too far gone. I was beyond help. I was destined to be bound to lust all my days. These were the fiery darts, the nuclear missiles, that the enemy had been shooting at me for so long that I completely believed them.

> *Brethren, I count not myself to have apprehended: but this one thing I do, forgetting those things which are behind, and reaching forth unto those things which are before, I press toward the mark for the prize of the high calling of God in Christ Jesus. (Philippians 3:13-14)*

Paul is telling his readers that he has not attained to something yet, but that he is living his life to attain this goal, or as he calls it: *the mark for the prize of the high calling of God in Christ Jesus.* What was this goal Paul had in mind? The answer is found in the preceding 12 verses.

Paul starts off this passage of scripture by encouraging his readers to do something: *Rejoice in the Lord.* The focus of our rejoicing is not in what we do, what we feel or what we think. We are to rejoice in the Lord. Paul continues by reminding the readers that if anyone wanted to boast about their credentials or achievements he probably could best them all. But, says Paul, all of those things are like dung. They have no worth. There is no time and place for anyone to hold on to dung. Any discussion surrounding bodily functions is a social faux pas. In our hygiene focused society we don't talk about these things. But God approaches this discussion in the Bible.

> *"You shall have a place outside the camp and you shall go out to it; and you shall have a stick with your weapons; and when you sit down outside, you shall dig a hole with it, and turn back and cover up your excrement.* <u>*Because the Lord your God walks in the midst of your camp, to save you and to give up your enemies before you, therefore your camp must be holy, that he may not see anything indecent among you, and turn away from you.*</u> *(Deuteronomy 23:12-14, RSV)*

In Deuteronomy 23:12-14 Moses, as instructed by the Lord, tells the Israelites that they are to have an instrument, in addition to their weapons, that would dig a hole and to bury the excrement. Why would God even discuss this? Because the Lord is among the camp. It is because He is holy and our daily life is to reflect the fact that the Holy God is in our midst. Symbolically, the camp represents our lives and hearts. We have to keep our hearts pure before the Lord. The Lord wants us to deal with those things that soil the heart. Those things, if left alone and not dealt with, will eventually bring sickness and death. The Lord wants to go fight for us, but unless we deal with the dark and dirty issues of our hearts, the Lord cannot go before us to save us and subdue our enemies.

Paul tells us that we are soldiers of Jesus Christ. We are fighting against principalities and powers of darkness. Our enemies are not of flesh and blood, they are spiritual. Our warfare is not with carnal weapons, but, he says, they are *mighty through God*. And in the middle of our constant warfare we have to take care of the cleanliness of our camp. We cannot presume to find freedom from our enemies if we are not willing to deal with our unclean hearts and hands. We have to deal with the dung on a daily basis.

Our battle with the flesh, with pride, and with works is constant.

Paul wanted us to see that, like dung, we have to deal with this flesh every day. Its chief desire is to be recognized and praised. It is pride at the core of it all. Our war is not with flesh and blood! We are actively engaged in warfare each day, and we must deal with the cleanliness of our camps – our hearts – daily! The living Almighty and Holy God lives within us and we need to prepare a place for Him to dwell. As we are called into submission and to resist the devil, God will give grace to the humble and He will resist the proud.

Paul is another Bible character that my wife said I was always like. He was a proud man who had to be humbled by the Lord. And when he was touched by the Lord his life was radically changed. She always believed that the Lord had a great calling on my life, but like Paul and his prideful ways, she knew that the Lord was going to have to humble me. And he has been doing that. Paul says this in Philippians 3, I haven't reached anything yet, but I am pressing on. What was it that he hadn't obtained yet? It was the resurrection power of Christ.

Paul knew that the full surrender of Christ led to the death of the cross. There was suffering that led up to that moment, and likewise, there is a suffering that takes place as we proceed toward that mark. Our suffering is marked by the battle and struggle between the spirit and the flesh. A struggle for the flesh to live and the spirit wanting to die to self. The culmination of that struggle was the cross. Paul wanted to be made conformable and surrendered to that life of Christ. But it is a very hard thing to do when pride wants to live. And I was, and have been, a very prideful and religious man – just like Paul.

I hate this way of living. I want to be rid of this old carnal nature that wants its own way. I can hear Paul's cry, *O wretched and miserable man that I am! Who will [rescue and] set me free from this body of death [this corrupt, mortal existence]?* (*Romans 7:24, AMP*) I have no hope in the ways of man. I have no hope in my own will and strength. I am no match for the devices of Satan against me. Alone against him I will lose every time. Woe is me when I think that I can do anything in my own strength against the enemy of my soul. His dark power is a thick shroud against me and covers my every way of escape. If I am to think that I have any chance against him I am already lost. My only hope is death. Death to self. Death to sin. Death to this world.

My life was rescued by the One who knew no sin. My life has been set free and ransomed by One who stepped down from heaven and took on this lowly human life so that I would find complete salvation in his complete victory against all the powers of darkness. And it was on the cross that He won the victory. And it didn't end there! When they thought He was dead and gone, He stepped into the kingdom of darkness and ripped the keys of hell and death from the devil and proclaimed that He was the victor! Jesus Christ overcame the power of hell and death to destroy sin's hold over you and me! And when He stepped out of the grave in resurrection power He brought me into that new life with Him. I am now alive, not because I did anything to gain victory – No! He did it all! He won my victory at the cross and then He made me an overcomer when He came to life! This is why Paul could now say *Thanks be to God [for my deliverance] through Jesus Christ our Lord! (Romans 7:25, AMP)*

This is what Paul wanted to attain to, this is what he wanted to apprehend – *the resurrection power of Jesus Christ.* This is the hope of my heart, this is the hunger and desire of my heart – to grab hold of the resurrection power of Christ in my life. And like Paul, I have to admit that I am not there yet, I have not yet apprehended that which Christ has won, but I press on toward it. I push forward day after day, and though there are days when I stumble or falter, I feel Him compel me to stand up and press on. He calls me day after day. Cleanse yourself in My Word! Call out to me and I will answer you and show you great and mighty things which you do not know right now (Jer. 33:3), but I will reveal and show you as you keep following me.

I look back at that time when I was on that road in my prideful ways, in my anger and bound in bitterness. I am reminded of His tender prompting in my heart that although it would be hard at times, although it would be difficult, and although I would hurt at times, I needed to have a determination and tenacity to keep putting one foot in front of the other that, no matter what I faced, *I was going to press toward the mark of the prize of the high calling of God in Christ Jesus!*

My wife saw things that only God saw in me. She saw the heart of Moses to lead the people out of slavery and she saw the zeal of Paul for a heart to pursue hard after God. I'm not done yet, but what is most encouraging and brings hope to my heart is that He is not finished with me yet. I have come far in my journey with Him. I may not be the man yet that God has destined for me to be, but I am not the man I once was, and for that I am truly indebted to Him.

Many years ago, before I was born, the Lord saw that I would need a strong woman, and not strong in her own ways, but strong in faith that the Lord is who He says He is. He knew that only a woman full of the Holy Spirit and full of wisdom would be able to walk with me in this holy calling.

Sonia, I love you so much. I thank God that you built a wall and dared not come down off of it until the Lord answered your prayer. I would be lost had you not stood in the gap. You are truly an intercessor of the Lord, a repairer of the breach. The Lord knew what He was doing when He put us together. Let's keep pressing on, my sweet. One day, we will walk, hand in hand, one foot in front of the other, in His everlasting Kingdom!

Beloved, keep pressing forward. Keep pressing on to the mark for the prize of the high calling of God in Christ Jesus. In other words, as He spoke to my heart that day out on the highway, 'Sometimes it's going to hurt, but no matter how far the journey may seem, just keep putting one foot in front of the other.' One day soon, just like my wife did for me on that dark and lonely road, He will come for us.

Epilogue

I never could have imagined how the Lord would meet us in the way He has. I look at my husband and I can see the joy of the Lord on his face. His face radiates. The words I hear him speaking now bring life and come from a yielded vessel.

Through the years, I have prayed for the Lord to part the Red Sea because I wanted to see wonders. He has parted the waters and we have walked over to the other side on dry ground. When the enemy's hoofs could be heard behind us He drowned the horse and rider in the sea.

He will fight for you. You will see His hand on everything if you look for it. His glory is seen everywhere. The bird in the tree. The wildflowers. The setting sun. The moon and stars at night. When things are hard, just look around and you will see Him. He knows everything about you and is working all things out for your good and His glory.

Serve him with all your heart and keep him as your first love. As long as you keep him in the forefront of all you do, you will prosper. Stay on your prayer wall and keep building. Keep your oil lamps burning. We shall soon meet the Lord in the air.

Notes

1. Times Square Church, *Because You Prayed | How to Make My Prayer Life a Reality*, Posted on March 10, 2024, YouTube, https://www.youtube.com/watch?v=NpGlXFg-QqY&t=400s

2. Jimmy Evans, *Marriage on the Rock* (Dallas, TX: Marriage Today, 2012)

3. John Kuypers, *The Peace Promise* (North Palm Beach, FL: Beacon Publishing, 2017)

ABOUT THE AUTHORS

Derek and Sonia McLeod have been married since 2010. As a blended family, they have seven children and several beautiful and wonderful grandchildren. They were ordained as ministers in 2011 with the *Independent Assemblies of God International (Canada)*.

Being a First Nation couple, Derek and Sonia have a love and passion to reach the Indigenous population of USA and Canada. Together, they are working toward opening a Christ-based outreach, mission and drug rehabilitation center focused on First Nation and Native American peoples.

Together they created the *My Nehemiah Wall* project with a vision to have a prayer wall in every Christian home globally.

Teach Me to War is Sonia's fourth title and Derek's first as an author.

OTHER TITLES BY SONIA MCLEOD
Rise Up My Beloved
100 Days Walking By Faith Daily Journal with Daily Devotions by Sonia
Prayer & Faith Annual Planner

***

For speaking arrangements, contact derekandsonia@gmail.com.
Other resources can also be found at www.mynehemiahwall.com

www.ingramcontent.com/pod-product-compliance
Lightning Source LLC
Chambersburg PA
CBHW011724150626
46549CB00019B/3288